111 9K

A CELEBRATION OF HEARTS

A Sampler of Heart Motifs for Quilting, Patchwork & Appliqué

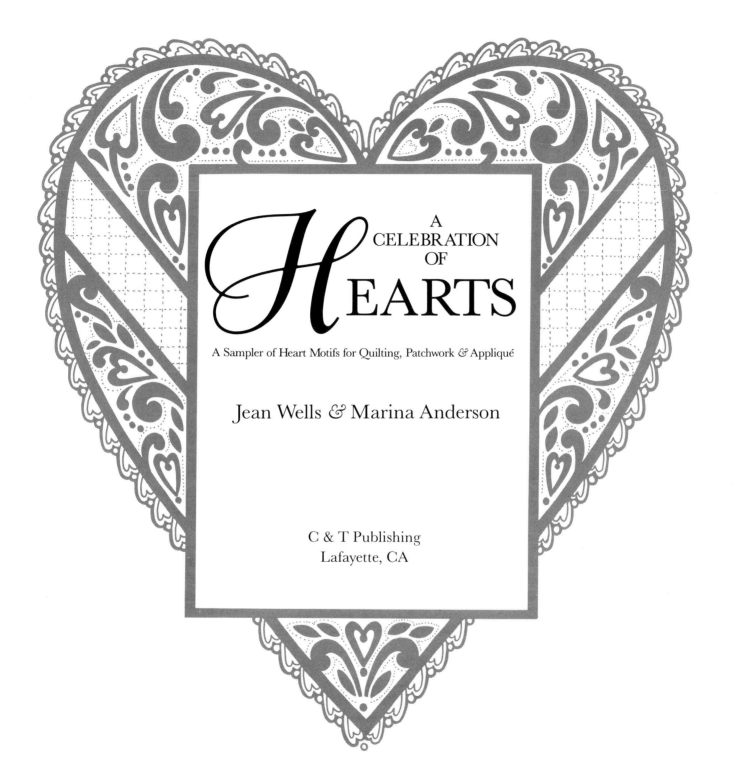

A CELEBRATION OF HEARTS

A Sampler of Heart Motifs for Quilting, Patchwork & Appliqué

Jean Wells & Marina Anderson

C & T Publishing
Lafayette, CA

Front cover photo:
Heartworks Sampler
Heartworks Sampler is a combined design effort by
both authors. Marina drew the quilt block concepts
with Jean designing and making the quilt top.
Heartworks Sampler was quilted by Mary Jahns.

Back cover photo:
Hearts and Vines
Designed by Jean Wells. Quilted by Mary Jahns

Photography by Indwar Sivanathan
Bend, Oregon

Project Coordination by Bobbi Sloan Design
Berkeley, California

Editing by Sayre Van Young
Berkeley, California

Typesetting by The Graphics Connection
Oakland, California

Published by
C & T Publishing
P.O. Box 1456
Lafayette, CA 94549

ISBN: 0-914881-22-1

Library of Congress Catalog Card No.: 88-72068

Printed in the United States of America

Contents

Heart Connections

Jean Wells   *Marina Anderson*

Thirteen years ago, Jean Wells opened her quilt shop, The Stitchin' Post, in Sisters, a tiny western town in Central Oregon. Marina Anderson was one of her first customers. ''Hearts connected'' at that time and have been connecting ever since. Marina became the resident artist at The Stitchin' Post, illustrating the class mailers and designing children's clothing.

Jean's premier published venture, *Patchworthy Apparel*, was illustrated by Marina. Since then, geographically, their friendship has had to stretch. Luckily, working from a distance has made them learn to communicate effectively. At times, they read each other's minds in their creative ventures.

Hearts have long been a favorite design motif for both artists. *A Celebration of Hearts* was launched many years ago in creative conversations. Both artists felt that collaborating on a publication would bring out the best of each one, creating a visual and learning celebration. So many ideas arose

during their work that truly only the very best are presented here.

Jean's extensive background dates back to junior high home economics teaching. Being a teacher at heart has lead her into the operation of her quilt shop and lecturing on the national quilt scene, along with producing three quilting books. Freelance design for magazines, national fabric manufacturers, and pattern companies has kept her in tune to innovative ideas.

Throughout Marina's career, hearts have danced across almost every design to leave her drawing table. She often refers to herself as a ''designer/heartist.'' For years, Marina worked for Yours Truly, Inc. *Crayon Creations* and *Crayon Design Workbook* are two successful publications from that period.

Since then, she has illustrated children's educational publications by Learning Boutique, designed cross-stitch leaflets for Leisure Arts, and created children's items for Oxmoor House. Look for a card line and fabric

designs from Marina in the near future.

Jean and Marina created the projects here to appeal to both the advanced and the novice heartmaker. There are even several no-sew or ''low-sew'' projects designed by Marina. Jean has written the majority of the manuscript as well as developed several innovative construction ideas. Marina's never-ending pencil not only illustrates and draws projects, but also supplies quotations.

A Celebration of Hearts is a gathering of many hearts. Families lend that ever-needed support that makes it possible to create at odd moments. Mary Jahns has again quilted her heart out on Jean's quilts; Marina's sister, Pat Epping, lent her special touch to the machine appliquéd projects. Cherie Beebe has been invaluable finishing pillows and machine quilting. Special quilts were loaned by Carol McIntyre, Nancy Taylor, and Nadine Thompson. Sayre Van Young's editing expertise is invaluable.

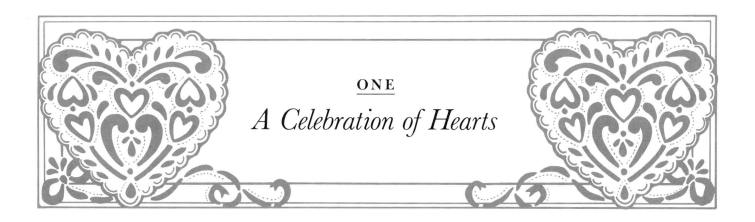

The Hearts That Bind Us
by Marina Anderson

...For every heart there is a season...a time...a reason....

Heart designs have always held a special and unique place in history. Their roots can be traced back an incredible twenty thousand years. Through those years, they have been displayed as universal symbols of life's most important events ...marriage, birth and death, friendship and romance, to name a few. Hearts adorned a vast array of items, from stoneware and furniture to documents and weather vanes. They embellished both functional and heirloom pieces, adding special meaning to all.

Combining hearts and quilting is a natural choice. Both possess a common link of past and present, of tradition and of possibilities. We are drawn to their deep yet essentially simple beauty. This beauty is not tinselled, fading with time, but speaks of memories of the heart, reflecting our personal tastes, life experiences, and feelings. In essence, through fabric, color, and design, we are creating our own message of life.

I once designed a picture of two quilters sitting back to back, each stitching away at opposite corners of a quilt. One quilter was very "old-fashioned," her piece reflecting a traditional look. The other had a contemporary flair. Her corner was pieced and quilted in quite another manner. As you visually followed the bound edges of the quilt corners, they joined to become one in the center. The title was "Quilting binds us all together." I feel this same kind of bonding in sharing my love for hearts. Regardless of style preference, sewing experience, or creative goals, we can all appreciate this many-faceted motif.

Jean and I are both incurable collectors of Heart Art. The wonderful thing about being a "heart collector" is that one is not limited by barriers of style. Hearts speak of every mood known. They effortlessly travel from room to room, easily becoming part of any decor.

My family has grown to accept my "heart condition." My children are used to heart graffiti on papers scattered by the phone and cheerfully recite to friends why mom's license plate reads "HART ART." Even my husband has become a victim. One day he called from his job site gloating that he could *finally* draw a heart. His "design by accident" was a lumber measurement, the numeral 13 jotted down on a board. When he picked it up and turned it a bit, it became a heart...of sorts. (To fully appreciate this, you would have to see his handwriting!) I can visualize you scribbling away, trying to figure how a heart can come of a numeral 13. You're on your way to the realization that design and inspiration can come from anywhere and everywhere!

My hopes are that through my illustrations, designs, and prose combined with Jean's matchless talents with fabric design and instruction, we will infect you with our "heart fever."

The Expanding Heart
by Jean Wells
Your mind is a "thought factory," busily producing countless thoughts each day. Being the creative person you are, you may sometimes feel overwhelmed with all the ideas and projects that spring forth. Sometimes, all that's needed is a way to manage those myriad ideas and project plans. I've found if I write it down, or

make a sample sketch, or cut swatches, then file them away, I've cleared a space in my mind. Then I'm free to use that space to its best advantage.

At the same time, by starting an idea file, you have become your own best resource. When you are stuck on a project or need a fresh idea, sort through your file. It's amazing how often I have been inspired by my stash of little notes and simple drawings.

Most quilters are visual people. They see the world and their environment as stimulation for creative ideas. Sunsets, flowers, shapes in architecture, all stimulate the imagination. And not all those exciting visions can be written down and filed. So tuck away in your mind the *energy* you feel when encountering an inspirational situation. Often in class a student will say, "I want to capture the feeling when I see—." Being able to feel on this level and translate that feeling to quilting is truly a gift. Develop your talents. Believe in your abilities. If you believe you can be successful in creating, you can.

Remember, your mind is like a bank account. Every day you make deposits of insights, ideas, possibilities. The "bank teller" is tremendously reliable and won't cross you up. If you ask, "Suggest some thoughts on color for my new wall quilt," she'll check the deposits you've made and come up with new, creative ideas. Not to belabor the simile, but to be sure your idea account doesn't get overdrawn, it's up to you to deposit these thoughts.

I find space away from my day-to-day environment opens up my mind to new thoughts. When I go on a short vacation, see some new countryside, or visit a gallery, my mind opens up in a new way. Usually, some hours later or even several days later, I'll have my notepad out, jotting down ideas for colors, or moods for a quilt, or shapes I want to translate into quilting. It's a wonderful time when that flow comes and you can't write ideas down fast enough. I've learned to make use of those moments and not be frustrated by the day-to-day hectic schedule my life sometimes takes.

My students often say, "Jean will find a way to save it," when their plan goes astray or there's a roadblock in their progress. Roadblocks are not negative to me. I see them as stimulators. They force you to draw on your own resources as well as encourage you to seek out ideas from others. During this decision time, you may need space to think or the project may need a rest for a day or two. Usually the solution comes when you have given yourself a break from being creative. Then check your file of jotted notes and fabric swatches. Check your internal file of memories and ideas. The answer will always come. You must believe that.

TWO

Project Planning

Are you ready to tackle a new project? Energy seems to rise as you begin something new. Perhaps it's the excitement of choosing and arranging fabrics into something personally satisfying. Those decisions are often a challenge. I want to reflect on some ideas that will help you in working through the projects in *A Celebration of Hearts*.

Inspiration

As I looked at the twelve designs individually in the sampler quilt, other projects developed. The heart shape sometimes is the stimulant, as in the quilt in Photo 11. When I finished the sampler block with the checkerboard grid, I wondered if I could put four hearts together and create a new design. I kept seeing the design in my mind in clear, bright pastels with the black-and-white checked grids. I could hardly wait to get my hands on the fabric and see it happen.

The same heart design inspired Marina in designing the sewing caddy (Photo 6). She called me one day describing this idea, and I asked her to send a sketch. From the sketch came the idea of making the seamed sections into separate pockets and layering them. (The

fun part for me was finding places for all the sewing tools I use!)

Throughout the book, I've tried to go beyond fabric selection and placement to describe the *inspiration* to you. I hope some of my thoughts will stimulate your mind and suggest imaginative possibilities for your projects. Remember, adjustments are usually necessary as you work through the creative process. Welcome the adjustments. They will lead you to new ideas.

Being creative to some seems second nature while others find it a little like being on roller skates for the first time. Being unsure and a bit off balance is part of the growth process in developing your imagination. I use a mental technique called the "What if" factor. It's a means of sharpening one's skills at finding possibilities. I take a design motif and ask, what if the hearts are overlapping...what if one is turned upside down...what if I add dimension by stuffing...and so on. The wonderful part about "what if" is there are no right or wrong answers; rather, it's a juggling process to find what *feels* right.

Theme

Hearts...hearts...and more hearts— they're the obvious theme of this

book. But look carefully at the photographs. Each setting was planned with a feeling in mind, a theme beyond hearts. See Photo 1, "Quiet Time Quilting." Fabrics were chosen with a soft relaxing mood. All the projects in that photo reflect a quietness in their choice of fabrics, in their design, in their arrangement. Now contrast this photo with "The Gifted Hand" (Photo 11), and its upbeat, bright pastel mood. The objects there suggest movement, energy, and gift giving.

To apply the concept of theme to your own project, think about where the project is to go, or who it is for, or what its function will be. These decisions will become parameters for your choice of design and colors. Oftentimes a particular fabric makes suggestions to me. The large cabbage rose fabric in the *Victorian Hearts* quilt just spoke to me. I felt buttons and ribbons were appropriate to carry out a Victorian theme. Always pay attention to details such as embellishments, binding, piping, quilting. They are the subtle touches that complete the mood.

Once a theme is chosen, repeat it. Repetition is a key word in my designing mind. When a color or piecing sequence works, repeat it. That doesn't mean it has to be repeated in the same scale, but the idea needs to reappear. Repetition of design and color will carry out the theme and give it unity. In my most successful projects, I've always felt like I was overdoing it—but that's when it works.

Look through the photos in this book. In each, we have tried to set a mood and carry it out with the projects, then reinforce it with props and accessories. See if you can "get" the theme before you read the photo caption.

Heart Shapes

From the geometrics of the "Checkerboard Heart" to the "Curved Heart," then to the more traditional heart in "At Home with Hearts," each and every heart shape has its own mood. The various shapes are explored here in a variety of projects that sets each one apart.

In each project, techniques are suggested that will make you successful in your heart construction. For example, the raised heart effect in the *Victorian Hearts* quilt was achieved by stitching through thin batting. I found it wasn't necessary to stitch the back of the heart after turning because it was to be attached to the quilt around the edges.

Approach each project with an open mind, using our construction suggestions but always on the lookout for the innovative technique that best suits the finished look *you* desire. Read Part Five, "Heart to Heart Basics," before you begin sewing, then refer to it if you need help.

Color and Fabric

Many books have been written on color, but I have found my own instincts and observations to be my best sources of ideas. Though my foundation in color concepts comes from art and home economics classes, my inspiration comes from the world around me—advertisements, art, greeting cards, nature, fabric, china.... An inspiring whirl of colors is available to us all. We literally only have to keep our eyes open.

As you approach color in doing the projects in the book, you won't always have similar fabrics available or you may not like the colors we've used. Here are some suggestions for successfully translating the color concepts.

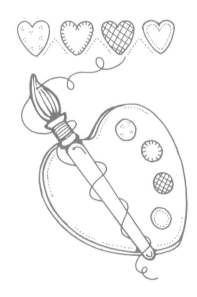

Observe the project, noting where we have used dark, light, or medium colors. If you duplicate the color range with your fabric choice, the design will balance. If you choose to experiment with lights and darks, cut out the fabric pieces, pin them on a wall, and observe them from a distance. Take time to study the design. You'll know if it works or not.

Now, take note of the scale of prints and plaids used. There are large florals, tiny plaids, swirly prints mixed with solids. A combination of varied-sized patterns works better for me than prints all of the same scale. In the sampler on the cover, the only print is the sashing. The blocks are solids and checks or plaids. Because of the small size of the blocks, some of the appliqué pieces are quite tiny. I was afraid of losing the design clarity if too many prints were used. My choice was to mostly use contrasting solids and accent with the plaids, but my theme for the colors came from the floral fabric. So pay attention to the scale of design when choosing the fabrics.

One caution: observe your fabrics from a distance. Fabrics change in complexity from a close-up view to a view from across the room. Many two-color prints have a textural feeling when seen from a distance. You don't even realize this until you step back to see the project.

Try to balance the fabrics, having mostly one color combination (lights and darks), then a lesser amount of another, plus an accent or sparkle. The sparkle makes it all work. The black background in the *Rainbow Hearts and Vines* quilt pulls all the colors together. It becomes the backdrop for the interaction of color and gives continuity to the design.

In the *Victorian Hearts* quilt, the buttons and ribbons are the accent. Sometimes piping becomes an accent; see the apron in Photo 8. A change in fabric texture can be an accent, too.

Finally, fabric and color choices are really a very individual matter. We all like certain colors, and tend to use them over and over. Push yourself to expand your color horizons. Take ideas from our combinations and add your own touch. Always remember to allow your projects to be as "color full" as possible.

THREE

*Everchanging Heart:
Heartworks Sampler*

HEARTWORKS SAMPLER

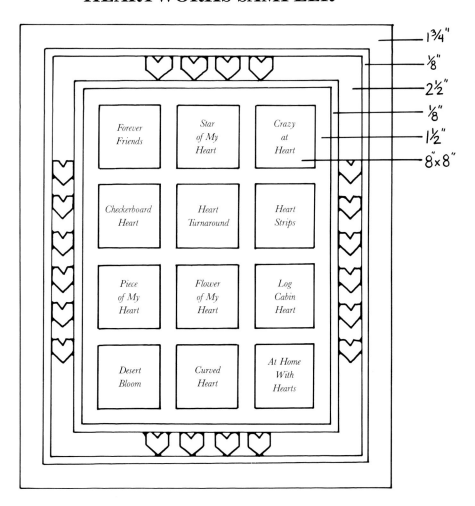

Forever Friends	Star of My Heart	Crazy at Heart
Checkerboard Heart	Heart Turnaround	Heart Strips
Piece of My Heart	Flower of My Heart	Log Cabin Heart
Desert Bloom	Curved Heart	At Home With Hearts

1¾"
⅛"
2½"
⅛"
1½"
8"x8"

*Finished size 38½" x 48"
3 blocks by 4 blocks
Each block 8" finished
(Front cover photo)*

Our hope in producing *A Celebration of Hearts* and in sharing our visions on design, color, and projects is that you will be inspired to create. Our goal is to spark—and sparkle—your imagination.

We began with a sampler of twelve basic blocks (drafted to an eight-inch finished size) as shown on the front cover. But every one of the basic blocks prompted another idea, another project. Each block can stand on its own as a pillow, or be repeated in a quilt, or become an appliqué on a project. These pages are filled with possibilities; each of the blocks has a section, detailing some of the additional projects. Plus, we added ''Heart Extractions,'' projects that take a single heart and repeat it. Remember, designs can be enlarged or repeated to meet your needs.

As you work through the book, you will see various styles of hearts. There are chunky Valentine hearts, and folk art hearts, long and pointed at the bottom. Some hearts have straight sides, as in Photo 11, so four hearts can fit snugly together; others have curvy sides. Experiment as you explore the world of heart magic. You'll find heart designs have a chameleon quality—they can take on a variety of looks.

We have included basic sewing information for all projects. Use the information in Part Five, ''Heart to Heart Basics,'' much like a dictionary, that is, when you need clarification of a technique or suggestion of a tool. Throughout, we hope to encourage, challenge, and inspire you as well as to give basic sewing instructions.

Heart shapes generate a special warmth. They represent the goodness in life. We hope to perpetuate that feeling in *A Celebration of Hearts.*

The various heart designs in the pages that follow have been tied together in the *Heartworks Sampler* with one floral fabric, plaids, and solids to present a total idea, a celebration of hearts.

A country French mood developed as I planned and sewed the designs. It's reflected in the mood of the colors as well as in the use of plaids. The floral frames all the designs and radiates a sense of continuity, giving unity to the total design. This is one project where I found I spent more time making decisions than actually sewing!

To pick your color palette for the quilt, note where light, dark, or medium colors are used, as well as where a plaid is used versus a solid. Your palette will be your own personal choice of fabrics so use the quilt as a frame of reference, not as a format to be followed precisely. As you become more and more involved with this project, your color decisions will come easier. Since the quilt isn't very large, scraps or ¼-yard pieces can be used. Listed below are the materials needed for the entire quilt.

Materials needed:
2½ yds. main fabric (floral)
⅛ to ¼ yd. each of pink background fabric (one light, one medium, and one dark)
⅛ to ¼ yd. each of green background fabric (one light, one medium, and one dark)
⅛ to ¼ yd. each of blue background fabric (one light, one medium, and one dark)
⅛ to ¼ yd. each of violet background fabric (one light, one medium, and one dark)
⅛ yd. of one plaid in each of the above colors
¼ yd. muslin
½ yd. ¼"-wide satin ribbon in each of the above colors
1½" x 7½" 14-count cream Aida cloth
Six old pearl buttons in various sizes
Six-strand embroidery floss in one of the above colors
1½ yd. 3 oz. bonded batting
thread to match

Instructions:
1. Follow the instructions in Part Four to construct twelve individual quilt blocks. Each block should measure 8½" x 8½" before seam allowances. Look at the cover photo for ideas on color placement.

2. To assemble the quilt, you first need to cut the following pieces:
main fabric (floral):
9 - 8½" x 2" - horizontal sashing
4 - 36½" x 2" - vertical sashing
2 - 30" x 2" - top and bottom sashing
4 - 3" x 8" - heart border
4 - 3" x 11½" - heart border
4 - 2" x 44" - last border
4 - 1½" x 44" - binding
1 - 40" x 50" - backing
narrow accent border:
8 - 1" x 44"
heart border:
Use the ''Pieced Heart'' pattern (see ''Heart Extractions'' in Part Four). Cut and piece 20 hearts in various solids for the border.

3. Assemble the blocks as shown on the following page, with a ¼" seam allowance. Press.

4. Add accent border around the edge. Press.

5. Heart border: Stitch four hearts together horizontally for top and bottom borders, then stitch six hearts together for vertical side borders. To each end of the horizontal borders, add a 3" x 8" rectangle of main fabric. To each end of the vertical borders, add a 3" x 11½" rectangle. Press.

Add horizontal borders to the top and bottom of the quilt, then add the side borders. Press.

6. Add second accent border around the edge. Press.

7. Add the last border to the top and bottom, then to the sides.

8. Mark the top for quilting. Again, follow the ideas in the cover photo or make up your own.

9. Layer the quilt; machine or hand quilt the layers together; add the binding (see Part Five for instructions).

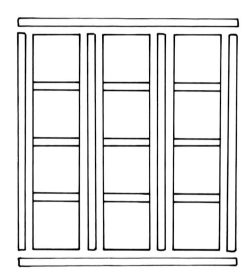

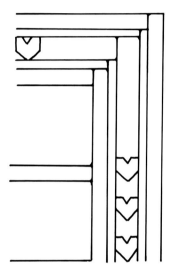

Border section

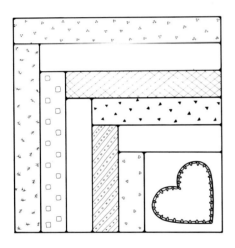

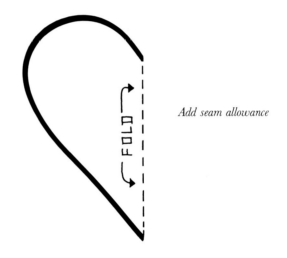

Add seam allowance

1. LOG CABIN HEART

(Back cover photo)

Strips are placed on only two sides of the center block in this Log Cabin variation. Colors can vary from light to dark radiating from the center as they do on the quilt on the back cover, or they can be placed randomly as they are in the sampler block. Try other arrangements of the blocks if you plan a quilt using this block.

All cutting measurements include seam allowance. As with all twelve of the sampler blocks, finished size is 8″ x 8″.

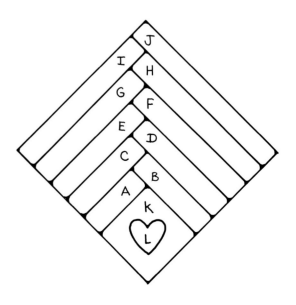

Materials needed:

Cut one piece of each of the following fabrics:

A - 1½" x 3"
B - 1½" x 4"
C - 1½" x 4"
D - 1½" x 5"
E - 1½" x 5"
F - 1½" x 6"
G - 1½" x 6"
H - 1½" x 7"
I - 1½" x 7"
J - ½" x 8"
K - 3½" x 3½"

small scrap fabric for heart
  appliqué
freezer paper for heart appliqué
thread to match

Instructions:

1. Heart: Cut a piece of freezer paper the size of the heart pattern. Press the waxed side of the paper to the wrong side of the heart fabric. Cut a scant ¼" seam allowance beyond the edges of the freezer paper.

2. Assemble the block. Using a ¼" seam allowance, stitch Piece A to K. Press the seam allowance toward A.

3. Continue the stitching process as follows, pressing toward each strip as it is added:
B to K - C to A - D to B - E to C - F to D - G to E - H to F - I to G - J to H

4. Position the heart in the center, as shown. Remember, there is a ¼" seam allowance at the bottom two corners.

5. Attach the heart following appliqué instructions in Part Five.

1A. Rainbow Hearts and Vines Quilt
Finished size 37½" x 37½"
Each block 6½" x 6½" finished
(Back cover photo)

Rainbow Hearts and Vines has a clear dramatic impact due to the use of solid colors. In each block, the colors move from light to dark beginning at the center. The intensity of the individual blocks changes across the quilt. The heart colors in the border coincide with the heart block colors.

Materials needed:
1¾ yd. background fabric
1¼" x 45"—solid colors in separate blocks—one strip of each color in each block (if you duplicate colors in blocks, then yardage will duplicate)
¼ yd. for hearts in blocks
3" squares for border hearts (for each heart)
⅝ yd. for vine and leaves
1⅛ yd. backing
1⅛ yd. 3 oz. bonded batting
string or yarn (long piece)
freezer paper for heart appliqué
thread to match

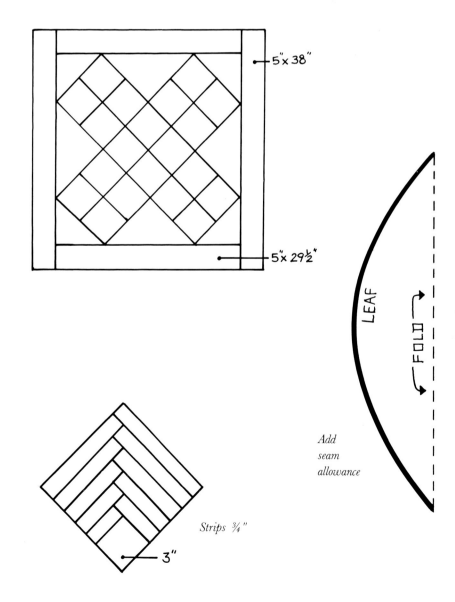

5" x 38"

5" x 29½"

Strips ¾"

3"

LEAF

FOLD

Add seam allowance

Instructions:

1. Cut the following pieces:
background fabric:
12 - 3½" x 3½" center squares
2 - 13" x 13" squares for corners. Cut across diagonally (see diagram).

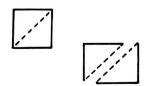

2 - 8" x 8" squares for sides, top, and bottom inserts. Cut across diagonally as shown.
2 - 5" x 29½" strips for top and bottom border
2 - 5" x 38" strips for side borders
4 - 1¾" x 40" strips for binding
Log cabin strips are cut 1¼"-wide from selected colors
hearts:
Make a total of 34 freezer-paper hearts.
12 - hearts for blocks. Press the waxy side of the freezer paper to the wrong side of the fabric.

Leave a scant ¼" seam allowance for turning under.
22 - colored hearts for border. Follow instructions above.
vines and leaves:
Cut 200 running inches of bias 2" wide.
Cut 16" leaves following the same instructions as for the hearts.

2. Using the "Log Cabin Heart" instructions, make 12 blocks.

3. Arrange the blocks, inserting corner and side pieces. Follow the diagram for sewing the quilt together. This is set diagonally. Stitch pieces together in Rows 2, 3, 4, 5. Connect Row 1 to 2, 2 to 3, 3 to 4, 4 to 5; press. Add the three other corner pieces; press. Add the bottom and top border; press. Add the side borders; press.

4. To make the tubing for the vine, stitch all the bias strips together, forming one long strip. Then fold the right sides together and insert a string or piece of yarn inside the tubing. Pin in place. Stitch across the end, as shown, then down the sides ¼".

Start pulling on the string, gently at first, to start the cord pulling through itself. Pull until the cord is turned. Clip off the end of the tubing where the string is attached. Press the tubing so that the seam is on one side.

5. Arrange the tubing around the quilt; look at the photo on the back cover. Where the two ends meet, tuck under the raw edges so the tubing butts together. Tack the tubing down.

6. Place hearts and leaves according to the photo, and hand appliqué them in place. (Follow the general instructions given in "Log Cabin Heart.")

7. Layer the quilt, machine or hand quilt, then add binding. For detailed instructions, see Part Five.

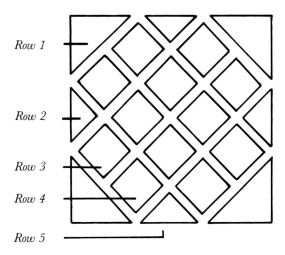

Row 1

Row 2

Row 3

Row 4

Row 5

2. PIECE OF MY HEART

As you look at this heart, you'll see it's actually a square in the center with the curved pieces added to make a heart shape. Within the square, any design could happen. On the sampler, I chose to quilt a heart in the center. A flower could also be appliquéd, as shown here. The diagonal lines can be pieced or quilted.

Materials needed:
scraps of fabric for the heart
8½" x 8½" square for background fabric
thread to match

Instructions:
1. Make patterns from the heart sections. Add ¼" seam allowance as you cut out the pieces.
2. Assemble. Add Piece A to the center piece, then Piece B. Add corner to C and C to the center. Add corners to D and D to the center. Press. Finally, add the two curved Es, to turn a pieced square into a "Piece of My Heart."
3. Using a ¼" seam allowance, stitch around the edge. This is the turning line for hand appliqué.

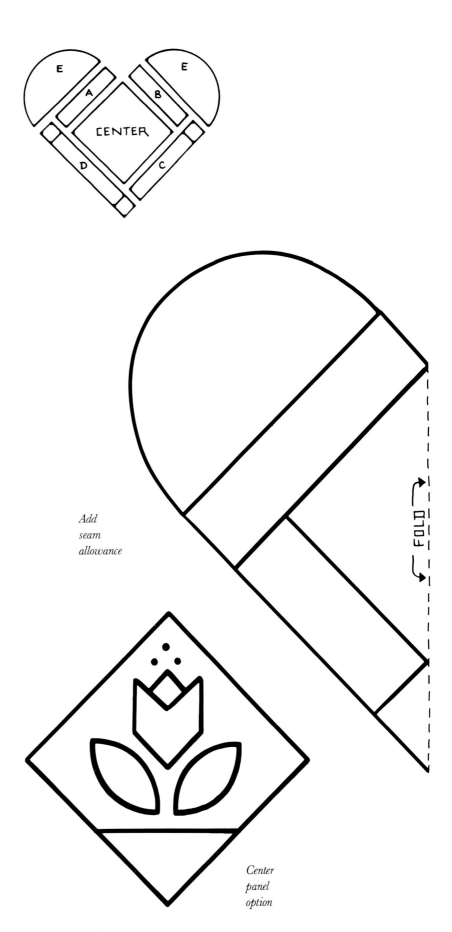

Add seam allowance

FOLD

Center panel option

2A. Square Bear/Bunny
(Photo 2)

Marina sketched the square bear and I transformed it into our stuffed version shown in Photos 2 and 11. Then the bunny idea popped into our minds. The bunny ears are 2″ x 8″. Otherwise, the bunny is just like the bear.

Any of our heart designs will fit on the bunny (here we use the "Piece of My Heart" pattern). Our "Heart of America" bear in Photo 2 uses several different fabrics with an Americana theme. In "Romancing the Heart" (Photo 7), the bunny is made of one fabric but is embellished with ribbons and lace.

This bear has been reduced in size to make it hand-holding size. In all the scenes, the fabric choices create a completely different mood ...and a completely different bear (or bunny!!).

Materials needed:
⅝ yd. one fabric or ⅛ to ¼ yd. pieces, if a variety of fabrics are used, for the bear and the heart
two buttons (for eyes)
six-strand embroidery floss
1 lb. Polyfil®
chopstick or unsharpened pencil
trimmings (optional)
3½″ x 42″ fabric for bow
ribbon (optional)
thread to match

Instructions:
1. Using the measurements shown, cut out the following pieces, adding ¼″ all around for seam allowance:
2 heads 5½″ x 7″
2 bodies 7″ x 7½″
4 legs 3½″ x 6″
4 arms 3″ x 3½″
4 ears 2½″ x 2½″

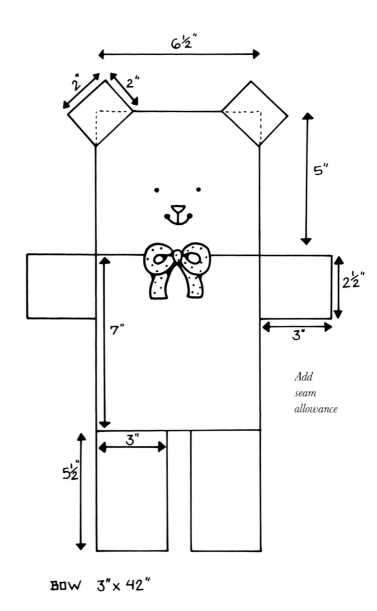

Add seam allowance

BOW 3″ x 42″

2. To form the arms and legs, place the right sides together of two pieces and stitch around the edges. Clip corners. Turn to the right side and stuff. When stuffing, push small amounts of Polyfil in at a time with the chopstick. Be sure to fill the corners.

3. For the body front, stitch the head to the body and attach one ear on each side of the head. Repeat for the back of the bear. Press.

4. Pin the finished arms and legs to the body of the bear. Place the right side of the back of the bear to the front. Stitch around

the edges, leaving an opening on the side for turning. Be sure to make square corners by leaving in the machine needle as you turn the fabric. Clip corners and turn to the right side.

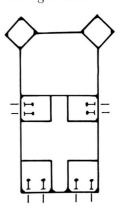

5. Stuff, using the instructions in Step 2. Hand stitch the opening closed.

6. Add the fabric bow or tie a ribbon around the neck. To make the fabric bow, take the 3" x 42" strip, place the right sides together, and stitch across the ends and down the side, leaving a 3" opening in the center to turn. Turn to the right side, and press.

7. The face consists of two button eyes, a tiny nose, and mouth. The nose is satin-stitched and the mouth is a backstitch (see the section in Part Five on "Embellishments" for diagrams of these stitches).

8. The "Piece of My Heart" pattern was used for the heart on the tummy. Once the heart is pieced, place it on the backing and put on 3 oz. bonded batting. Stitch around the edge and turn. Then hand quilting can be added. Look at Photos 2, 7, and 11 for ideas.

2B. Garland of Bears
(Photo 9)

Here "Piece of My Heart" bear has been reduced in size to make a bear garland; or it can be used singly as a gift or package topper. Hearts join each bear together.

Materials needed:
scraps of a variety of solid fabrics, including:
6" x 6" scrap for each bear's head/body
3" x 8" scrap for each bear's arms
5" x 8" scrap for each bear's legs
3" x 6" scrap for each bear's ears
5" x 11" scrap for each heart
⅜" x 10" strip for each bow
3" x 6" scrap black fabric for vests
1⅓ yd. black single-fold narrow bias tape
black embroidery floss
½ lb. Polyfil℠
Wonder-Under Fusible Web℠
1 yd. black ⅜"-wide grosgrain ribbon
chopstick or unsharpened pencil
thread to match

Instructions:
1. Cut (for each bear):
2 head/body pieces 2½" x 4¼"
4 legs 1⅜" x 1⅞"
4 arms 1⅜" x 1½"
4 ears 1⅛" x 1¼"
two vests—black fabric, 2" x 2½"
(cut V in one 2½" side of each vest; cut other 2½" side to come to a point in the center)

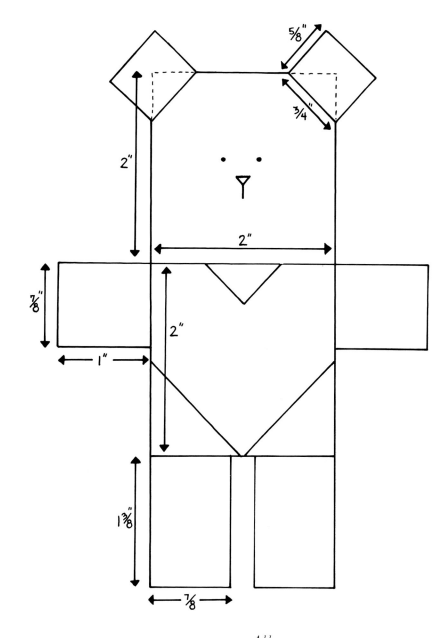

*Add
seam
allowance*

six hearts—two of each color
three bows—each ⅜" x 10" strip

2. Using the Wonder-Under, fuse the vest to the bear body. The bottom point of the vest should be ¼" from the bottom edge of the body. Machine appliqué the top and bottom edges of the vest.

3. Embroider each bear face with black embroidery floss.

4. Follow the instructions in ''Square Bear/Bunny'' to complete the bear.

5. Sew hearts, leaving an opening in the side. Notch curved edges. Turn and stuff. Whipstitch opening. With black floss, embroider a running stitch approximately ⅜" in from the edge of the heart. Top with a fabric bow.

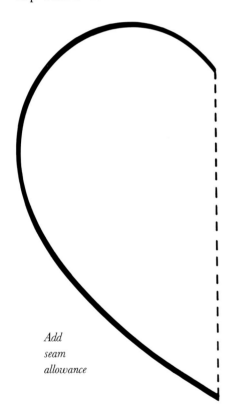

*Add
seam
allowance*

6. Whipstitch bears and hearts together. Tie bows in ⅜" strips, and tack or glue one on each heart.

7. Cut two pieces of grosgrain ribbon 18" long. Attach them to the hearts by hand, making a loop as they are stitched on.

2C. Piece of My Heart Hot Pad
(Photo 8)

This heart-shaped hot pad has diagonal pockets on each side for the hand to fit inside; it's a clever gift idea.

Materials needed:
8" square Fabric #1 (cream print)
⅛ yd. Fabric #2 (blue print)
8" square Fabric #3 (midweight cotton for back)
¼ yd. Fabric #4 (rose plaid)
scrap Fabric #5 (rose print)
scrap Fabric #6 (light green solid)
scrap Fabric #7 (rose solid)
scrap Fabric #8 (dark green solid)
¼ yd. Thermolam®
Wonder-Under Fusible Web®
thread to match

Instructions:
1. Cut:
Piece A—one of Fabric #1
         one of Fabric #3
         two of Thermolam
Piece B—four of Fabric #2
         two of Thermolam
Piece C—one of Fabric #8
Bias strip: Make bias strip from three 8" square pieces of Fabric #4.

2. Press the heart front to crease the center line. Make a prairie point using Fabric #7. Cut appliqué fabric (with Wonder-Under), fuse in place, and machine appliqué. Sew the triangle (Fabric #8) just below the appliqué, and baste to the bottom edge of the heart.

3. Lay the heart front, the two layers of Thermolam, and the heart back together, and baste.

4. Sides: Lay two pieces, right sides together, with one piece of Thermolam under, and stitch the straight edge. Turn, press, and baste the curved edge. Repeat with the other side. Lay side pieces on the heart, and baste.

5. Cut a 2"-wide bias strip. Bind the edge of the hot pad. Stitch down the center of the hot pad, through all thicknesses.

2D. Piece of My Heart Apron
(Photo 8)

A striped fabric highlights this apron and appliqué design. The heart is strip-pieced with a machine appliqué floral design in the center. Almost any of the heart designs in this book could find a place on the bib of the apron.

Materials needed:
1 yd. Fabric #1 (blue print—apron)
1 yd. Fabric #2 (lengthwise striped print)
⅓ yd. Fabric #3 (cream striped print—bib)
5" x 5" scrap Fabric #4 (cream print—heart—Fabric #3 could be used)
6" x 6" scrap Fabric #5 (dark rose print)
¼ yd. Fabric #6 (light green solid)
⅓ yd. Thermolam®
⅔ yd. ⅛" cording
white topstitching thread
blue embroidery floss
Wonder-Under Fusible Web®
thread to match

Instructions:
(Using a copy machine, enlarge the heart design to 7" high.)
1. Cut:
apron skirt—one 28" x 36" piece of Fabric #1
apron sash—four 2½" x 36" pieces of Fabric #1
apron neckties—two 4" x 34" pieces of Fabric #2
apron bib—one 9¼" x 18" piece of Fabric #3
bias strip—three 8" x 8" pieces of Fabric #6
9" x 9¼" piece of Thermolam®

heart:
Fabric #1— cut two of Piece A
             cut one of Piece F
Fabric #2—cut two of Piece D
Fabric #4—cut one of Piece C
Fabric #5—cut two of Piece B
             cut one of Piece E
             cut one of Piece H
Fabric #6—cut two of Piece G

2. Sew the heart pieces together. Cut the appliquéd pieces, and fuse them in place. Machine appliqué. Lay the heart on a piece of Thermolam, and cut to fit. Baste around the edges. Stitch in ditch along all seams. Outline stitch around the appliquéd pieces. Mark triangle points on fabric. With topstitching thread, stitch along the triangle lines and just inside the machine appliqué. Pull on the bobbin thread to bring the topstitching thread ends to the back side.

3. Make a bias strip using three 8″ squares of Fabric #6. Encase cording with 1″-wide bias strip, using the zipper foot of your sewing machine. Baste around the heart, beginning and ending at the top V of the heart.

4. Baste Thermolam piece to half of the bib piece. Place heart on bib (above Thermolam), center it, and pin. Stitch in ditch around cording, tucking seam allowance under heart. Embroider French knots on the center square of the heart.

5. Fold each necktie strip in half lengthwise with right sides together. Beginning 9″ up from the ends, stitch along the long edges. Pivoting at the corners, continue stitching along the short ends. Clip the seams and corners, then turn the neckties right side out through the 9″ opening. Press.

6. Open out each 9″ opening of necktie pieces. Clip the seam allowance to stitching. Pin the opened edge of one necktie to one side edge of the bib, right sides together. Stitch. Repeat with the other necktie piece. Press seams towards each necktie.

7. Turn neckties to inside. Fold under the seam allowance at the opening, and slipstitch them closed.

8. Hem the bottom and side edges of the apron skirt. Stitch close to the edges.

9. Gather the upper edge of the apron skirt to 13″.

10. Pin the short ends of two sash strips right sides together. Stitch, then press the seam open. Repeat this process with the remaining two strips.

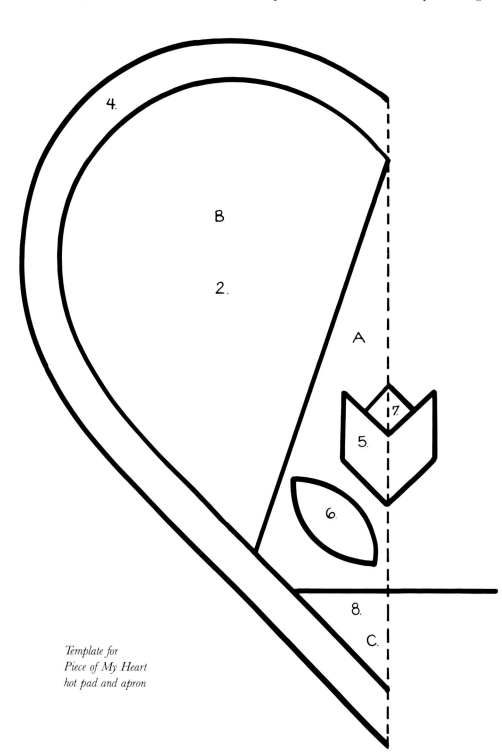

*Template for
Piece of My Heart
hot pad and apron*

11. Fold strips in half crosswise to find the center. Mark. Open out sash strips.

12. Pin one sash strip to the lower edge of the bib with right sides together, centering bib on sash. Stitch.

13. Pin sash strips right sides together, sandwiching the bib in-between. Stitch along edges, leaving an opening in the center of the edge not attached to the bib.

14. Clip seams and corners. Turn sash right side out, and press.

15. Pin the skirt to the sash with right sides together at opening. Stitch. Clip seams, and press towards sash.

16. Turn under seam allowance along the opening on the apron and slipstitch the opening closed.

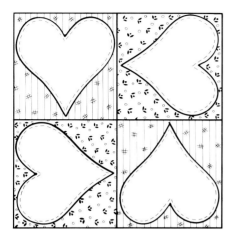

3. HEART TURNAROUND

This block is simply four squares with appliquéd hearts. The hearts turn at each corner to form a spiral effect. So many fabric possibilities come to mind: for example, bright hearts on a black background, or a crazy quilt kind of look using lots of scraps. Machine appliqué of hearts could make this an everyday useable quilt.

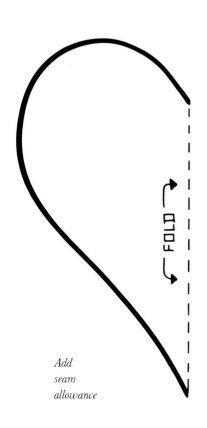

Add seam allowance

FOLD

Materials needed:

four 4½″ x 4½″ squares of four colors for background
four 4″ x 4″ squares of four colors for hearts
four 4″ x 4″ freezer paper for heart appliqué
thread to match

Instructions:

1. Cut four hearts from freezer paper from the pattern shown. Then press the waxy side down to the wrong side of the heart fabric. Cut out each heart, adding a scant ¼″ seam allowance.

2. Hand appliqué one heart to each of the 4½″ x 4½″ squares, then stitch the four squares together.

3A. Seamly Woman Pincushion
(Photo 1)

You'll never lose your pincushion again with this project! The words "Seamly Woman" are backstitched on Ribband, then attached to this decorative as well as functional pincushion.

Materials needed:

7″ cross-stitch ribbon (Ribband®)
two 2″ x 7″ fabric for piping
14″ x 7″ fabric for cushion
⅛ lb. Polyfil®
picture frame (5″ x 7″ opening)— no glass
5″ x 7″ mat board
Olfa knife
tacky glue

glue gun
strapping tape
chopstick or unsharpened pencil
felt-tipped pen
thread to match

Instructions:

1. Trace one of the hearts from "Heart Turnaround" to the wrong side of the mat board (center the heart widthwise, and leave a 2½″ space from the heart tip to the bottom of the mat). Cut out the heart using an Olfa knife. The cut does not need to be perfect since the cushion will hide minor cutting imperfections.

2. With a felt-tipped pen, trace a heart for the cushion to the wrong side of the fabric, using the mat heart you just cut out to enlarge the pattern. Cut two, and sew their right sides together (¼″ seam allowance), leaving approximately 1½″ opening for Polyfil stuffing. Turn right side out, and stuff lightly.

3. On the wrong side of the mat, push the cushion partially through the heart opening. It should puff out approximately ¾″. Secure it to the mat back using strapping tape on all edges.

4. Band: Backstitch the wording to Ribband. Fold both pieces of fabric piping wrong sides together lengthwise. Glue to the back of Ribband edges so that ¼″ piping is exposed. Place the band piece lengthwise across the bottom portion of the mat, leaving approximately ⅜″ from the bottom of the band to the bottom of the mat.

SEAMLY WOMAN

5. Insert the finished mat into the frame. Layer 5" x 7" cardboard (usually included with each new frame) to cover the back. Secure as per manufacturer's instructions included with the frame.

3B. Amish Turnaround Pillow
(Photo 9)

The Turnaround Heart block has been enlarged to 6" x 6". Hearts banded together and topstitched in black create an Amish mood. Hearts are machine appliquéd.

Materials needed:
8" x 8" scraps, each of eight different solid-color fabrics
⅛ yd. 45"-wide black fabric (add more if used for backing)
½ yd. Thermolam®
¼ yd. 3 oz. bonded batting
16" x 16" square pillow back
black topstitching thread
Wonder-Under Fusible Web®
½ lb. Polyfil®
thread to match

Instructions:
1. Cut:
four 6½" x 6½" pieces of four different fabrics
four heart shapes of four remaining fabrics
two 1½" x 6½" strips of black
three 1½" x 13½" strips of black
two 1½" x 15½" strips of black

2. Fuse the hearts to squares, using the Wonder-Under, and machine appliqué in place. For a smooth appliqué, stitch first with a looser zigzag, then finish with a tight satin-stitch. Press.

3. Join squares 1 and 3 with a 6½" strip. Repeat with squares 2 and 4. Press the seams toward the squares. Next, sew on the 13½" strips. Again, press the seams toward the squares. Last, sew the 15½" strips to the top and bottom. Press the seams toward the squares.

4. Lay the pillow top on a piece of Thermolam. Pin. Stitch in ditch around each square, leaving one outer side of each square unstitched.

5. Cut four heart shapes of batting. Trim batting ¼". Insert the batting hearts directly under the appliquéd hearts. Stitch remaining sides of squares.

6. Using topstitching thread, stitch around each heart, just inside the machine satin-stitch. You may need to change to a heavier-weight needle. Stitch slowly and carefully, "walking" the needle with the hand wheel around curves. Pull bobbin threads and use a pin to pull the topstitching thread ends to the back. Knot.

7. Baste around the outside edges of the pillow top. Trim excess Thermolam.

8. Follow the instructions in "Heart to Heart Basics" for finishing the pillow.

4. CRAZY AT HEART

Crazy patch just couldn't be left out of the sampler heart quilt. The charm of crazy patch is everlasting. Little treasures of fabric and trim come together in various shapes to make up the crazy quilt design.

We have provided templates for our heart patch, but once you've tried crazy patch, your own needle and imagination will carry you to new crazy patch endeavors. Let your trims, laces, and old linens find a home in crazy patch.

Materials needed:

scraps of fabrics, muslin, ribbons, and trims
1½″ x 7½″ 14-count cream Aida cloth
embroidery floss
thread to match

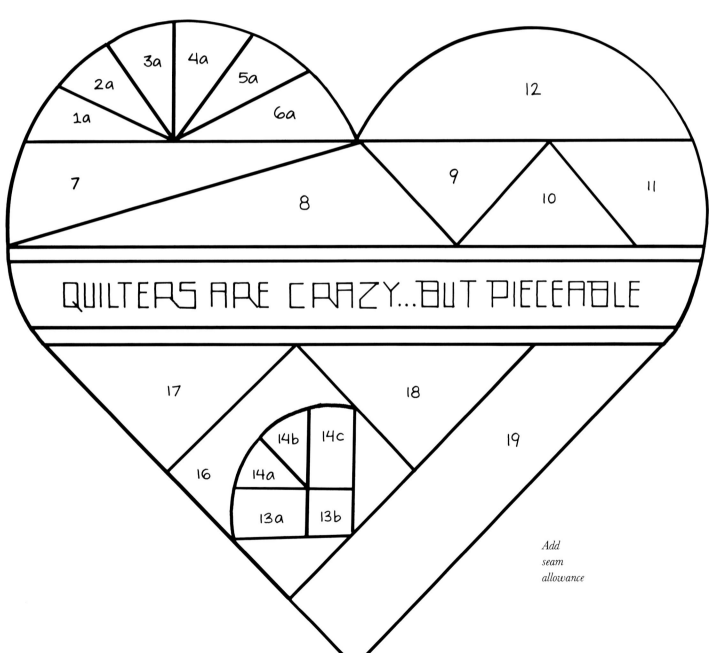

QUILTERS ARE CRAZY...BUT PIECEABLE

Add seam allowance

Instructions:

1. Using the heart shape pattern, add ¼″ seam allowance to the outer edge, and cut out the shape from muslin.

2. Make templates from the heart sections, adding ¼″ seam allowance. Place them in order on a table. Cut the fabrics right side up.

3. Piecing of the heart is done in sections. Stitch Piece 1a to 2a to 3a to 4a to 5a to 6a. See the diagram. Press. Stitch Piece 7 to the section just completed. Add 8, then 9, 10, 11, and 12. Press. The top part is now completed. For the bottom section, stitch Piece 13a and b together. Set aside. Then stitch 14a, 14b, and 14c together. Now stitch 13ab and 14abc together. Add 15a, then 15b. Piece 16 will have to be added with hand stitching. Press. Add 17 to the section just completed, then continue by adding Pieces 18 and 19. If you're planning on adding to Piece 19, do it now.

4. Backstitch the letters for "Quilters Are Crazy—But Piece-able" on the Aida cloth. Be sure to center the letters. Use three strands of embroidery floss. Press.

5. Trim ⅛″ off the top and bottom of the Aida cloth.

6. Center the Aida cloth on the heart. Place ¼″-wide ribbon over the top and bottom of the raw edges. Machine stitch both edges.

7. Topstitch ¼″ away from the raw edge around the heart on the seam line.

8. Place the heart on the background fabric, and hand appliqué it in place.

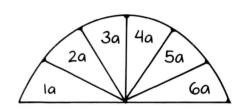

4A. Crazy Patch Quilt
Finished size 20″ x 20″
(Photo 2)

An old crazy patch quilt inspired this design. The old quilt had touches of the faded yellow that worked as an accent and made the reds and blues work. Simple diagonal hand quilting 1″ apart in the background gives the quilt continuity.

Materials needed:
1⅓ yd. main fabric
⅓ yd. muslin
palette of scraps for crazy patch
⅝ yd. 3 oz. bonded batting
½ yd. backing
thread to match

Instructions:

1. Cut from the main fabric the following pieces:
1 - 18″ x 18″
2 - 2″ x 20″
2 - 2″ x 24″
Cut muslin pieces:
2 - 1½″ x 18″
2 - 1½″ x 20½″
4 - hearts using the heart shape

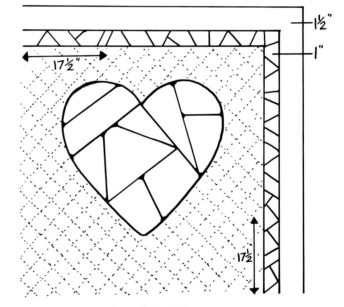

Crazy Patch Quilt

from "Piece of My Heart"

2. Follow the crazy patch instructions given in "Crazy at Heart," and piece the four hearts and borders. The fabric is sewn to the muslin. Press. As you position the fabrics, use the accent sparingly. The heart should be mostly one color (blue, in this case) with some red and a tiny amount of yellow.

3. Stitch around the edge of the hearts, ¼″ from the edge. Position the four hearts evenly on the 18″ x 18″ background, remembering there is a ¼″ seam allowance allowed. Hand appliqué.

4. Add the pieced borders to the top and bottom, then to the sides. Press.

5. Add the main fabric borders to the top and bottom, then to the sides. Press.

6. This quilt is hand quilted with a diagonal grid 1″ apart. Mark the quilt before layering.

7. Layer and baste the quilt, then hand quilt.

8. Trim the backing and batting to within ½″ of the outside border edge on the front. Turn under the front border ¼″ and flip to the back of quilt. Hand stitch.

4B. Crazy Heart Fused Print
(Photo 7)

Tiny pieces of fabric have been fused to create this project. Ribbons, laces, and trims are added with glue.

Materials needed:
⅓ yd. 1⅛″-wide Ribband®
14″ x 18″ base fabric
½ yd. Wonder-Under Fusible Web®
fabric scraps
ribbon and lace scraps
buttons, beads (optional)
embroidery floss (optional)
thread to match
picture frame (16″ x 12″ opening)
Olfa knife
tacky glue
glue gun (optional)
tape
tracing paper

Instructions:
1. Enlarge the crazy heart motif (using a copy machine) to approximately 10¼″ length by 11½″ width. Trace each pattern piece, numbering both the master pattern and each individual piece. On the finished piece, various smaller sections are combined into a larger piece for variation.

2. Embroider your desired wording, if any, or leave it blank.

3. Apply Wonder-Under to your chosen fabrics, following manufacturer's instructions. Cut each pattern piece and pin it together with the pattern to keep track of proper placement.

4. Begin placement on the basic fabric by laying the ''point strip'' centered and 3″ from the point to the bottom of the fabric. Work your way up, referring to the master pattern as you go. Make adjustments, if needed, so the heart is centered.

5. Fuse to base fabric, following manufacturer's instructions. Glue on embellishments (ribbons, lace, buttons, etc.) using a glue gun or tacky glue.

6. Cut the mat board using the Olfa knife. Cover with the finished crazy heart block following manufacturer's instructions. Mat if desired. Mount in frame.

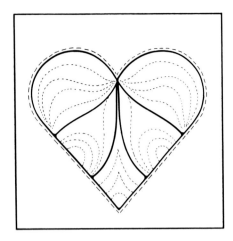

5. CURVED HEARTS

The curved heart can stand alone as it does on the sampler or it can be combined with other hearts. The center (Section B) is designed so that when the heart is combined with a second heart, it appears as a part of a ribbon. Curves in a simple form are surprisingly easy to piece and add interest within the heart shape.

Materials needed:
two 5" x 5" squares for Section A
two 5" x 5" squares for Section B
one 3½" x 7" piece for Section C
one 8½" x 8½" square for
    background
thread to match

Instructions:
1. Make pattern for Sections A, B, and C. Remember to cut C on the fold. It's the center of the heart. (Seam allowance of ¼" can be added to the pattern piece when making it, or it can be added when the fabric is cut.)

2. Place patterns on the fabric and cut. Mark notches lightly with a pencil on the wrong side of the fabric.

3. Pin Section A to B, matching notches. Stitch ¼" from the raw edge. Press seam allowance toward Section A. Repeat.

4. Pin Section B to C, again matching notches. Stitch ¼" from

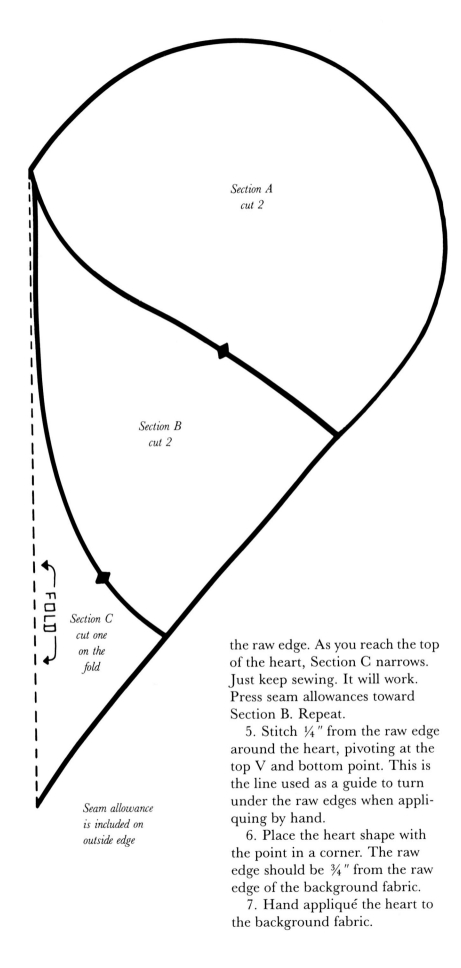

the raw edge. As you reach the top of the heart, Section C narrows. Just keep sewing. It will work. Press seam allowances toward Section B. Repeat.

5. Stitch ¼" from the raw edge around the heart, pivoting at the top V and bottom point. This is the line used as a guide to turn under the raw edges when appliquing by hand.

6. Place the heart shape with the point in a corner. The raw edge should be ¾" from the raw edge of the background fabric.

7. Hand appliqué the heart to the background fabric.

5A. Victorian Hearts Quilt
Finished size 29" x 33"
(Photo 5)

The large cabbage rose floral fabric was the inspiration for *Victorian Hearts*. My love of ribbons and buttons definitely found a place in this design.

Curved hearts lend the mood to the background fabric to create the theme of soft Victorian curves. Ribbons and buttons embellish the quilt and add the accent needed; I used old pearl buttons found at a junk store, then added a few special heart buttons.

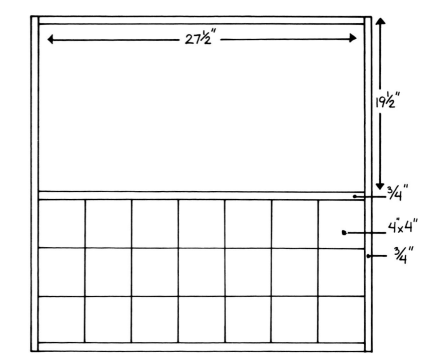

Materials needed:
1¼ yd. main fabric
¼ yd. each of six coordinating prints and solids
⅓ yd. frame fabric
1½ yd. 3 oz. bonded batting
1½ yd. backing
2 yds. of five or six ribbons varying in width from ⅛" to ⅞"
buttons
thread to match

Instructions:
1. Cut the following:
main fabric:
1 - 28½" x 20½"
3 - 4½" x 4½" squares
8 hearts
coordinating prints:
32 hearts
17 - 4½" x 4½" squares
frame fabric:
9 - 1¼" x 44" strips
bonded batting
16 hearts
Using three of the coordinating fabrics, cut the pieces for curved hearts, adding ¼" seam allowance.
2. Stitch the curved hearts together. Stitch ¼" from the outer edge around each heart. Join the three hearts together (see Photo 5).
3. Center the hearts on the main fabric and hand appliqué in place.

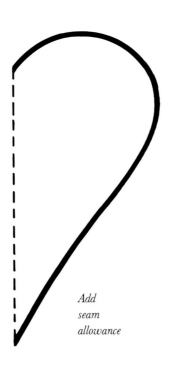

Add seam allowance

4. Add a strip of frame fabric to the top and bottom edge.
5. Arrange three rows of seven squares each. Stitch the rows together, press the seams, then join the rows. Press.

6. Add to the previous piece. Add frame fabric to the bottom and sides.
7. To make the hearts, refer to "Dimensional Hearts" in Part Five.
8. Place the hearts randomly on the squares. Tack in place.
9. Mark the quilting lines in the top section of the quilt.
10. Layer the quilt, baste the layers, and hand or machine quilt along the marked lines.

11. Place the ribbons on the hearts randomly. The ribbons create a third dimension and add special interest. Then add the buttons. Stitch through the buttons twice and knot after each button.

Layer the buttons at times to create dimension. Space your center of interest buttons.

12. See Photo 5 for ribbon and button placement on the lower hearts.

13. Quilting is done randomly in the squares. It is not as noticeable as in the section of the heart just above.

14. Add the last of the accent strips to bind the quilt.

6. FLOWER OF MY HEART

As you look at this drawing, visualize all the quilting lines drawn in. Basically, it is two heart shapes with flower appliqués. The ribbon and buttons are added for dimension. This design lends itself to quilting as seen in the pillow in Photo 1.

CENTER

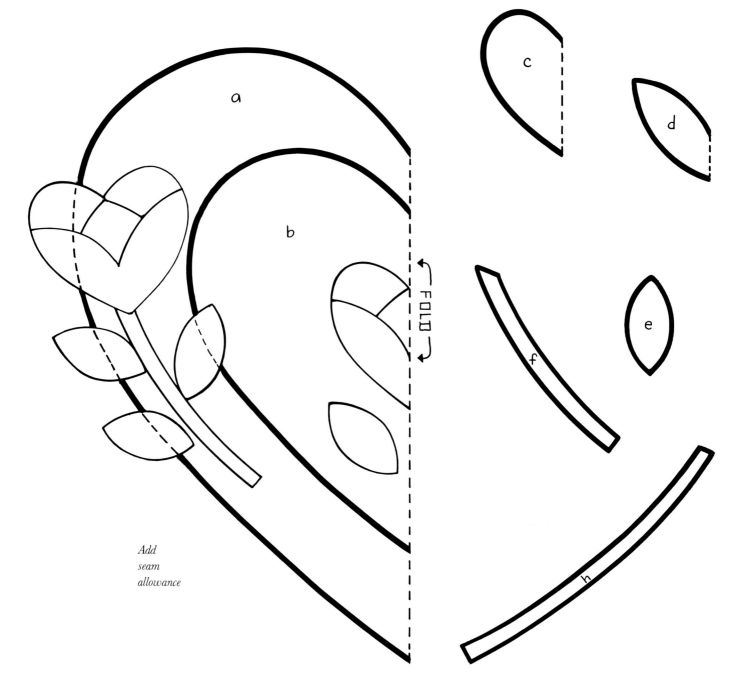

c

d

a

b

FOLD

f

e

Add seam allowance

h

Materials needed:
8" x 7" fabric for larger heart
4¼" x 5" fabric for smaller heart
8½" x 8½" fabric for background
scraps for flowers, leaves, and
    stems
½ yd. ⅜"-wide ribbon for bow
six old buttons
thread to match

Instructions:
1. Make patterns and cut the
two hearts, remembering to add
seam allowances.
2. Cut the flowers and stems,
adding freezer paper to the backs
of the fabric.
3. Machine stitch ¼" from the
edge around the hearts, then clip
at the center. Hand appliqué in
place on the 8½" x 8½" square
background fabric.
4. Stitch stems, leaves, and
flowers in place.
5. Tie a bow in the ribbon and
tack it in place. Position the ends
of the ribbon and tack them in
place with French knots.
6. Add buttons; look at the
drawing for placement.

6A. Flower of My Heart Pillow
Finished size 14" x 14"
(Photo 7)

When Marina had finished sketch-
ing this design and I first saw it, it
just said, "Quilt me." I can see
an entire cloth quilt quilted in this
design. It's so soft and feminine
looking.
I chose an embossed muslin to
quilt the design on. I enlarged
the design on the copy machine
until it measured 9" high, then
transferred it to the muslin and
hand quilted. Cording is added
to the edge. I purchased 1¾ yd.
of cording and cut fabric on the
bias 1" wide to measure 60" in
length, then made my own covered
cording (see "Embellishments"
in Part Five).

Materials needed:
two 14½" x 14½" fabric
one 14½" x 14½" muslin
one 14½" x 14½" 3 oz. bonded
    batting
1¾ yd. ⅛" cording (optional)
thread to match

Instructions:
1. Trace the pillow design on one
piece of the 14½" x 14½" fabric.
2. Layer the pillow design on
the batting, then place it on the
muslin. Use large basting stitches
to secure the layers.
3. Hand quilt the design. For
further instructions for making
cording and finishing the back of
the pillow, see Part Five.

6B. Flower of My Heart Appliquéd Pillow
Finished size 12" x 12"
(without ruffle)
(Photo 1)

The floral design just seems to say
pastel, so French country fabrics
were chosen. The design was
machine appliquéd, then machine

quilted to give dimension. The
"Flower of My Heart" pattern
was used.

Materials needed:
⅓ yd. fabric for ruffle
⅜ yd. for background fabric
    (#1, cream solid)
8" square for heart
    (#2, light rose print)
6" square for heart
    (#3, cream print)
fabric scraps for heart flowers
    (#4, dark rose solid)
⅛ yd. fabric for stem and leaves
    (#5, light green solid)
fabric scraps for base of flower
    (#6, dark green solid)
3" x 9" fabric for prairie point
    (#7, light blue solid)
⅔ yd. ½"-wide cream lace
⅜ yd. 3 oz. bonded batting
Wonder-Under Fusible Web®
¾ lb. Polyfil®
thread to match

Instructions:
1. Cut two 13"-round pillow
pieces from Fabric #1. Cut appli-
qué pieces:
Fabric #2—one piece A
Fabric #3—one piece B
Fabric #4—three pieces C
Fabric #5—ten pieces E
            one piece F
            one piece G
            one piece H
Fabric #6—three pieces D
2 - 6" x 45" strips for ruffle

2. Cut appliqué pieces (with Wonder-Under). Make three prairie points from Fabric #7. Position the large heart in place first and fuse with the lace underneath. Position the remaining pieces and fuse together. Machine appliqué. Press. Mark quilting lines.

3. Lay the pillow top on the square of batting and pin together. Machine stitch on the quilting lines, beginning with the stitching around the smaller heart, then stitching inside the smaller heart. Next, stitch around the large heart, then do the remaining stitching.

Baste around the edge of the pillow top. Trim batting.

4. Follow instructions for ruffles in Part Five. Back the pillow with the second 13"-round pillow piece, and stuff it with Polyfil. Then close the opening by hand.

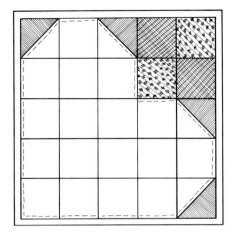

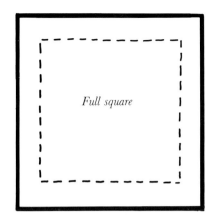

Full square

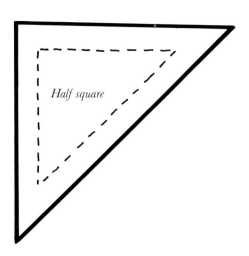

Half square

7. CHECKERBOARD HEART

Checkerboard hearts are created from a grid of squares. This grid is 1½″ finished. The burgundy quilt in Photo 2 is a 1¾″ grid. Since you are working with a grid, it is very simple to enlarge or reduce the heart shape. Notice the difference between Carol McIntyre's wall quilt (Photo 10), done in all solids shading from light to dark and one print, and the block in the sampler done with many fabrics. Looks definitely change with fabric choices.

A nine-patch grid was created for the four hearts in Photo 2. Then all-burgundy solids finish the top sections of the heart. The border incorporates the grided heart in the sampler border. The squares can be cut separately using a template, though a rotary cutter can simplify and speed up the process.

Materials needed:
lots of fabric scraps
thread to match

Instructions:
1. Add ½″ seam allowance to each square (¼″ for each edge). An example is 1½″+½″=2″. This is the grid used in the sampler.

2. Cut:
heart fabric—17 2″ squares

background—four 2″ squares

corners—four half-squares of background and heart fabric

background—two strips ¾″ x 7½″
two strips ¾″ x 8½″

3. Piece the rows first and press seams. Then stitch each row together. See diagram.

4. Add the ¾″ x 7½″ strips to the top and bottom. Press. Add the ¾″ x 8½″ strips to the sides. Press.

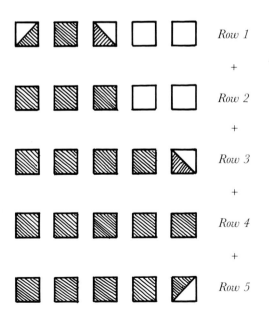

Row 1
+
Row 2
+
Row 3
+
Row 4
+
Row 5

(Text follows color plate section.)

1. Quiet Time Quilting. A "pieceful" setting brings together just what our hearts desire—time to quilt! A simple heart motif captures each floral design in Nadine Thompson's quilt. The *Seamly Woman* pin catcher is within reach for the chairside quilter and a decorative delight when not in use. Softly romantic is the mood for *Flower of My Heart* pillow and matching table cover with the bunny adding whimsical charm.

2. Heart of America.

A touch of America is displayed by Square Bear with his *Piece of My Heart* tummy. The patchwork flag pillow carries on with stuffed stars at the corner. Crazy patch, an old American favorite, is featured using a new piecing technique. Repeated *Checkerboard Hearts* is seen on the wall quilt.

3. Desert Bloom.

Nancy Taylor transformed a basically simple design of free-form hearts into a dramatic statement through the use of color and multiple borders. Big in size and big in color and design describes the *Desert Bloom* pillow, also made by Nancy.

4. A Welcome Heart. Christmas colors sing year-round in this two block quilt design *Star of My Heart*. Appliqué and basic pillow construction create a home design that warms the heart.

5. Victorian Hearts.
Grandmother's button box spills
onto the curved pieced hearts in
this wall quilt. Hearts are slightly
stuffed to produce a dimensional
effect. Clusters of crazy patch
hearts embellish the fabric-covered
band box.

6. Soft at Heart.
Touch the heart with lace and gentle
curves to achieve this romantic yet
vibrant look. Quilting on contrasting thread highlights the gentleness
of the design. Both function and
beauty are found in the tabletop
heart sewing caddy. Pockets, pincushion, and spool holders are all
combined in one.

7. Romancing the Heart. The bouquet of hearts pulls together a feeling of friendship and giving. *Forever Friends* repeats this in a nostalgic manner utilizing the traditional heart and hand motif. *Flower of My Heart* quietly blooms in quilting with button and ribbon ornamentations. The fusible crazy heart becomes embellished art through a no-sew technique.

8. Cooking with Heart. Bring a heart flavor into your kitchen with multiple use of heart design. Simple fusing of fabric finished with a frame creates a unique recipe card holder. A decorated band box is suitable for giving goodies or as a part of a kitchen heart display. A French country mood comes across with the use of striped and floral fabrics combined with the *Piece of My Heart* design. The potholder combines design and function as does the bordered towel topper. French bread and wine fit perfectly into this *Checkerboard Heart* tote.

9. Amish Hearts.
Heart turnaround pillow is machine
appliquéd and bordered in black
for an Amish look. Square Bear is
reduced in size and combined with
stuffed hearts to become a garland.

10. More Amish Hearts.
The shading of the checkerboard hearts adds dimension
and intrigue to Carol
McIntyre's quilt. The hand
and heart motif makes a
creative statement in this
no-sew project.

11. The Gifted Hand. Giving from the heart with gifts from the hand.... Here square bear finds bright new colors to lighten anyone's day. The cute and cozy slippers are purchased and decorated with the watermelon heart motif. No-sweat pieced and appliquéd sweatshirt is a perfect example of ''wearable heart.'' Hearts join together to form a fun graphic look in the quilt.

7A. Checkerboard Hearts Wall Quilt
Finished size 26" x 26"
(Photo 2)

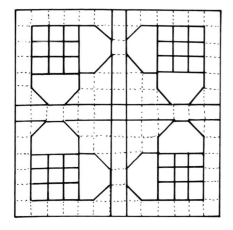

The center of the heart is treated as a nine-patch using only one print in this checkerboard heart design. A 2" grid was used for the hearts.

Materials needed:
1 yd. background fabric
⅓ yd. for heart tops
scraps for nine-patch design in hearts
¾ yd. backing
¾ yd. 3 oz. bonded batting
two 1½" x 26" strips binding
two 1½" x 28" strips binding
thread to match

Instructions:
1. Using the ''Checkerboard Heart'' instructions, piece four hearts. Press. The heart squares are 2" finished so cut all squares 2½". The fabric is arranged so that the prints form a nine-patch. Then the top edges of the hearts are solid colors. See Photo 2.

2. Once the hearts are finished, add enough pieced background fabric to go between the hearts and around the edges.

3. Layer and baste the quilt, then machine quilt.

4. Add the 1½" x 26" binding strips top and bottom, and the 1½" x 28" binding strips for the sides. Flip to the back and turn under for binding. Hand stitch.

7B. Checkerboard Heart Wine Tote
(Photo 8)

A bottle of wine and loaf of French bread fit nicely in this great gift tote. Or you could use it as a purse or for carrying small quilting projects. A lightweight canvas used for the body of the bag gives it shape. Scraps can be used for the heart and to add a country mood. All solids would create another theme. Handles are elastic. The fabric just gathers nicely around the elastic, creating a flexible handle.

Materials needed:
½ yd. 45"-wide heavyweight cream-colored fabric (or lightweight canvas) (tote body)
½ yd. dark mauve print (for lining, cording, and heart pieces)
⅛ yd. each of six prints in mauves and blues (heart pieces)
⅓ yd. Thermolam®
2⅛ yds. ⅜" cording
⅔ yd. ⅞"-wide elastic
4½" x 7¾" piece of cardboard (tote bag)
thread to match

Instructions:
1. Cut:
cream fabric:
9" x 28½" piece (tote body)
2 - 4½" x 22½" pieces (tote sides)
2 - 2½" x 18" pieces (straps)
dark mauve fabric:
3 - 8" x 8" pieces (for bias strip)
9" x 28½" piece (lining)
checkerboard heart:
Cut prints into 2" x 2" squares and half-squares for piecing

(finished squares for hearts will be 1½" x 1½")

2. Using the ''Checkerboard Heart'' instructions, piece two hearts. Press.

3. Lay the pieced hearts at either end of the body and lining pieces. Cut the body and lining to fit the shape of the top of the hearts. Pin the heart pieces to the body. Hand appliqué the bottom of the hearts to the body. Baste around sides and top.

4. Cut Thermolam to fit the body; baste the two pieces together along the stitching line. Find the center point of each body side and clip to the stitching at 2" on either side of it. Fold each side piece in half crosswise, and press. Baste around the sides.

5. Make bias with three 8" x 8" pieces of dark mauve. Cut into 1⅞"-wide strips. Piece together to make a 75" strip. Cover cording. Trim to ¼" from stitching. Sew cording around the edges of the body, starting and ending by overlapping the ends at the center of one side. Clip and pivot at corners. Clip the top V of the hearts and the round V at the bottom slightly when stitching.

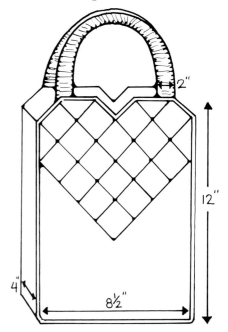

6. Sew the side pieces to the body, right sides together. Match the top of the side to the top of the body side. Pivot at clips.

7. Fold the strap pieces in half lengthwise and stitch the long edges. Turn them right side out and press. Insert a 12″ length of elastic in each strap. Stitch across the ends. Sew the straps securely in place at the tops of both hearts, raw edges even.

8. Sew the lining to the body at the tops of the hearts, right sides together, stitching from where the sides are joined. Turn the tote inside out. Pin the lining to the body. Turning the lining edge under ¼″, whipstitch one side to the body, with the seam toward the body. Insert the cardboard bottom. Whipstitch the other side. Turn the tote right side out, and press.

7C. Amish Hearts Quilt
by Carol McIntyre
Finished size 38½″ x 79″
(Photo 10)

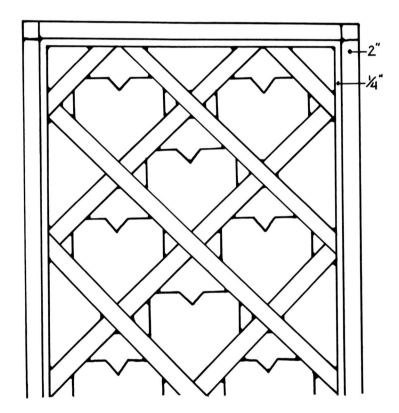

Heart Block: 8¾″ x 8¾″

This *Amish Hearts* quilt was designed and made by Carol McIntyre while taking a class from Lawry Thorn at The Stitchin' Post. Carol's choice of the dark teal for the top right-hand portion of the heart combined with the lights and darks in the balance of the hearts creates a shadow effect within the hearts.

The same colors are combined in a ¼″ strip in the border. The heart grid is 1¾″ finished squares.

Materials needed:
4 yds. black fabric (background, backing, and binding)
¾ yd. teal fabric
¼ yd. each of eleven solid-colored fabrics
¼ yd. one print fabric
2¼ yds. 3 oz. bonded batting
thread to match

Instructions:
1. Using the "Checkerboard Heart" instructions, construct ten checkerboard heart blocks. Blocks will measure 8¾″ when finished.

2. Cut the following pieces:
corners: two blocks 16″ x 16″ cut diagonally
side corners: two blocks 8″ x 8″ cut diagonally
piecing strips: seven strips 3″ x 44″

3. Piece the blocks diagonally as shown. Then add corners.

4. Borders: Cut one strip 2½″ x 44″ from each fabric used in the hearts. Stitch together and cut across ½″. Connect and add to the quilt. Cut six black border strips, each one 3½″ x 44″. Add to the top, bottom, and sides of the quilt.

5. Cut six 1½″ x 44″ strips for binding.

6. Layer the quilt, then machine quilt. Add the binding to the edges.

8. FOREVER FRIENDS

This block represents the everlasting friendship we have experienced. It's the beginning block in our quilt. In the quilt, the border is not pieced. The geometric corners are quilted instead. The little points were eliminated in the sampler quilt but added as prairie points in the pillow in Photo 7.

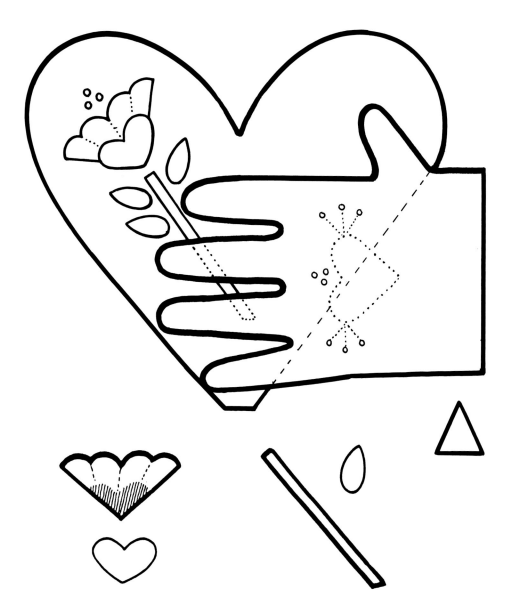

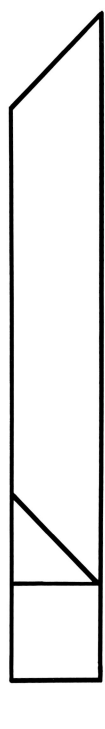

*Add
seam
allowance*

FOREVER FRIENDS

Materials needed:
6½" x 6½" fabric for center block
5½" x 5½" fabric for heart
3" x 4" fabric for glove
1½" x 45" fabric for border
1½" x 8" fabric for border
fabric scraps for flower, stem,
    and leaves
½ yd. ¼"-wide ribbon
six-strand embroidery floss
thread to match

Instructions:
1. Cut the center block 6½"
x 6½". Cut one border strip 1½"
x 44".
2. Add the border strip to the
center block. Press.

3. Cut the heart shape, adding
¼" seam allowance. Stitch ¼" from
the edge around the heart. Clip
at the center. Hand appliqué in
place.
4. To make the glove, trace the
shape on the wrong side of the
fabric lightly with a pencil. Place
the fabric on a lining fabric.
Machine stitch along the pencil
lines. You may need a smaller stitch
on the machine to be able to get
around the fingers. Leave the glove
open at the end. Clip and turn to
the right side.
5. Using the freezer paper
method, stitch the flower, stem,
and leaves in place.

6. Place the glove on the heart
and tack it in place.
7. Tie a bow with the ribbons.
Stitch it in place. Position the ties
and tack with French knots.

8A. Forever Friends Pillow
Finished size 12" x 12"
(without ruffle)
(Photo 7)

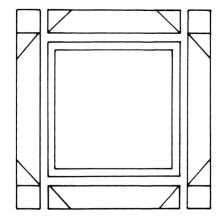

Cream and white is one of my
very favorite color combinations.
I wanted a white glove so the
remainder of the design was
planned around that color decision. It's always a challenge to
create enough contrast in a cream
and white palette.

Materials needed:
1 yd. main fabric and ruffle
two 8" squares medium cream
    fabric

¼ yd. white fabric
⅓ yd. darkest cream fabric
ceramic heart button (optional)
½ lb. Polyfil®
½ yd. ½"-wide picot-edge ribbon
embroidery floss to match one of
    the darker colors
thread to match

Instructions:
1. Enlarge the ''Forever Friends''
pattern to 12" x 12", using the copy
machine method.
2. Using the pattern, cut out the
pillow center and border. Add
¼" seam allowance to all pieces.
3. To piece borders, see the
diagram.
4. Trace ''FOREVER
FRIENDS'' in pencil on the
fabric. Backstitch the letters.
5. The center heart and glove
are made by placing two edges of
fabric right sides together and
stitching around the edge. Leave
the glove opening on the end and
the heart opening on the side.
Clip curves. Turn to the right
side. Press.
6. Make prairie points following
instructions in Part Five. Start

with a 2" square. Cut 18 squares.
7. Position the heart and glove,
and pin in place. Then slip the
prairie points under the heart.
Hand stitch in place.
8. Tie a bow in the ribbon. Tack
in the center, then position the
ribbon tails and tack with French
knots.
9. I used a heart button and
ribbons for the flower shape held
by the hand. On the glove, a heart
can be quilted or a button sewn on.
10. Ruffles: Cut three strips 6" x
44". Stitch the three strips together
lengthwise. Fold in half. Press.
Gather edge and position on pillow
top. Finish the pillow according
to instructions in Part Five.

8B. Framed Forever Friends
(Photo 10)

What a terrific gift for a friend!
Most people can find a special spot
for a print. The fabrics are all
fused, then framed. True friendship makes a full circle around
the frame.

Materials needed:

13" x 16" base fabric
1⅔" yd. ¼"-wide ribbon
½ yd. Wonder-Under Fusible Web®
embroidery floss (optional)
thread to match
two 2¼" x 8½" fabric pieces for strips
two 2¼" x 11½" fabric pieces for strips
four 2¼" x 2¼" squares for corner strips
two 3" squares for corner triangles
picture frame (11" x 14" opening)
11" x 14" needlework foam mounting board
tacky glue
strapping tape
tracing paper
tubed fabric paint (optional)
felt-tipped pen (optional)

Instructions:

1. Enlarge the "Forever Friends" heart motif to 6½" (at the widest part of heart width) using a copy machine.

2. Cut a 13" x 16" base fabric rectangle. Apply Wonder-Under to your chosen fabrics. Cut strips and corner squares. Fuse them to the base fabric, making sure they're straight and even with all base fabric edges.

3. Trace hand and heart motif pattern pieces, and cut fabrics. Cut 21 triangles, ¾" (width) x ¾" (height). Lay them on the base fabric, making sure the design is centered, in this order: outside strips and squares, corner triangles (square cut diagonally), glue ½" ribbon to triangles, heart flowers in corners, center heart, flower, glove, triangles. Fuse. Refer to the enlarged pattern for placement guide.

4. Cut a 2¾" piece of ribbon. Glue it to the edge of the glove. Add ¼" ribbon at borders.

5. Lettering: Embroider or print (using felt-tipped pen or tubed fabric pen). Refer to Photo 10 for order of placement.

6. Optional: Using tubed fabric paint, outline the edges of design, as desired.

7. Mount on foam mounting board following manufacturer's instructions. Place in frame, and secure.

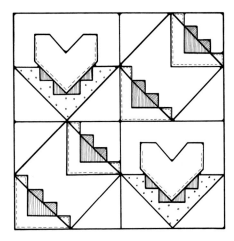

9. DESERT BLOOM

This design looks complicated, but it's not when you break it down into simple pieces. The tops of the hearts in Section 2 are actually prairie points. The "Desert Bloom" design radiates a southwest feeling as you can see in the pillow Nancy Taylor did in Photo 3.

Two sections are made, then joined together to form the total block. Take note where I used darks and lights. Contrast is needed if the hearts are to show. I used my rotary cutter to cut all the pieces once I made my templates.

Materials needed:
⅛ yd. of fabric for each color
   choice
thread to match

Instructions:
1. Make templates of all pieces, adding ¼″ seam allowance, and label each.

2. Look at the diagram for piecing sequence. Press after each seam.

3. Join the four sections when completed.

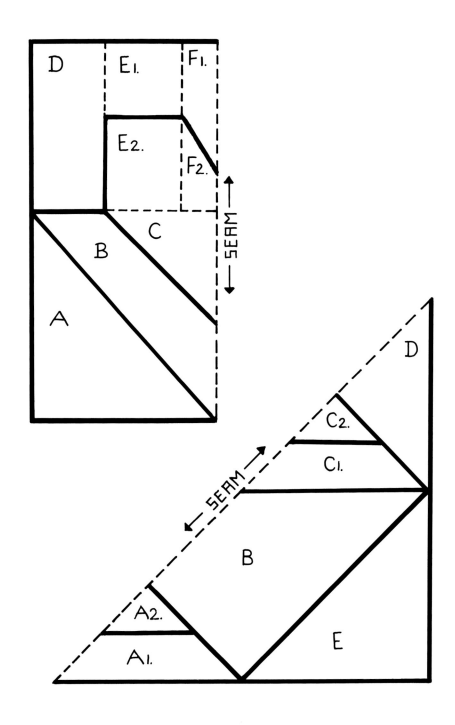

Section
1

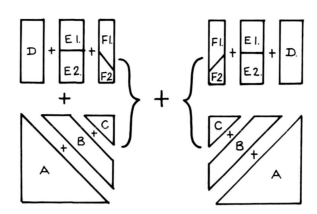

Section
2

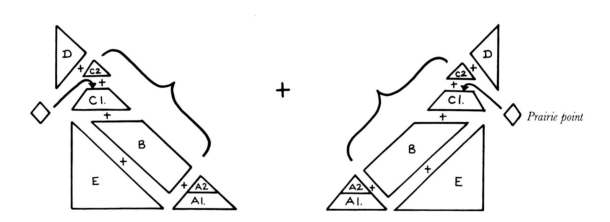

Prairie point

9A. Floor Pillow

Finished size 20" x 20"
(Photo 3)

"Desert Bloom" was the perfect geometric combination for this floor pillow. Nancy Taylor made the pillow in colors to match her *Freehand Hearts* quilt.

Materials needed:
⅓ yd. black fabric
¼ yd. taupe fabric
¼ yd. each of three shades of green fabric
¼ yd. light rust fabric
¼ yd. grape fabric
¼ yd. magenta fabric
20" x 20" fabric for back
1½ lbs. Polyfil®
thread to match

Instructions:

1. Enlarge the "Desert Bloom" block to 8" x 8"; then four of them will make a 16" square pieced design.

2. Follow the "Desert Bloom" instructions to piece the pillow top.

3. Out of the magenta fabric, cut four strips 1" x 16". Add these to the edges of the pillow.

4. Out of the darkest green fabric, cut four strips 2" x 20". Add these to the edges of the pillow.

5. Follow instructions in Part 5 for finishing the pillow.

10. STAR OF MY HEART

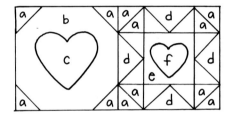

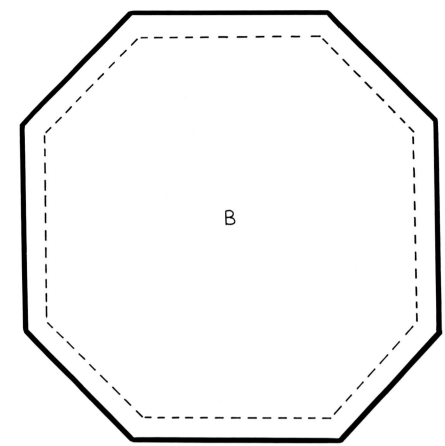

Seam allowance included

*Add
seam allowance
to hearts*

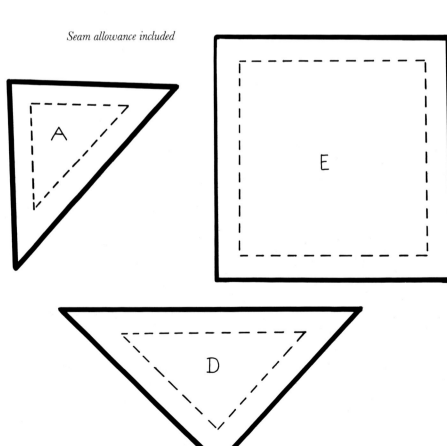

Two traditional quilt block patterns, "Sawtooth Star" and "Snowball," are combined here to form the repeat in this design. A larger and smaller heart are added to create movement within the design. The book *A Dozen Variables*, by Marsha McCloskey and Nancy Martin, raised my interest in combining blocks to create a new design. Hearts are a natural addition to the center blocks.

The sampler block is small so the triangles are more difficult to stitch. In the *Star of My Heart* quilt, the quilt is scaled larger. The triangles or half-square can be made from strips stitched together. The wall quilt in Photo 4 was done this way.

As you look at the mockup of the blocks, you need to think about colors. When Pieces A and E are the same fabric in the "Sawtooth Star" block, they give a star feeling.

The corner pieces are background. When combining the two blocks in a larger quilt, the corner pieces will create diagonal movement. Before I begin on patterns such as this, I go to a copy machine, make several copies, then paste them up. I get out my colored pencils and experiment. In fact, the lap quilt is the fourth color experiment in a set of five.

The templates have seam allowances added. Once colors are determined, cut out the amount needed.

Materials needed:
fabric scraps
thread to match

Instructions:
1. Cut:
2 - Piece B
2 - Piece C
8 - Piece D
16 - Piece A for star
16 - Piece A for star corners
8 - Piece A for snowball
2 - Piece C (add seam allowance after freezer paper has been pressed to wrong side of heart fabric)
2 - Piece F (add seam allowance, as above)

2. Stitch 4

Stitch 1

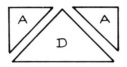

Stitch 1

Stitch 1

Stitch 2

Add the above section.

Stitch "Star Block" to "Snowball," then join the two sections together.

3. Center the hearts and hand appliqué.

10A. Star of My Heart Wall Quilt
Finished size 36" x 60"
(Photo 4)
23 star blocks,
22 snowball blocks
Each block 6" finished

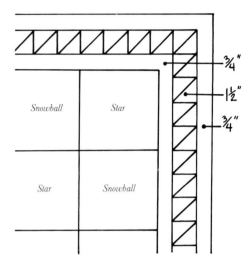

This design seemed to need that scrap quilt look. My stash of reds and greens goes back ten years as I've always wanted a quilt in this combination of colors. The softer green was chosen instead of cream for the center block to add sparkle. As I worked on this quilt, the reds and greens became richer and richer. I'm going to make a special place on my living room wall for it instead of just saving it for Christmas.

The border grew out of the repetition of the blocks. My first plan was to continue the half-square triangles all around, but they competed too much with the movement in the body of the quilt. The black band helps to contain the movement in the quilt and adds a nice frame.

Materials needed:
If you're using scraps, cut up what you have, but you'll probably need additional fabric. If you choose to use the same fabric in the same

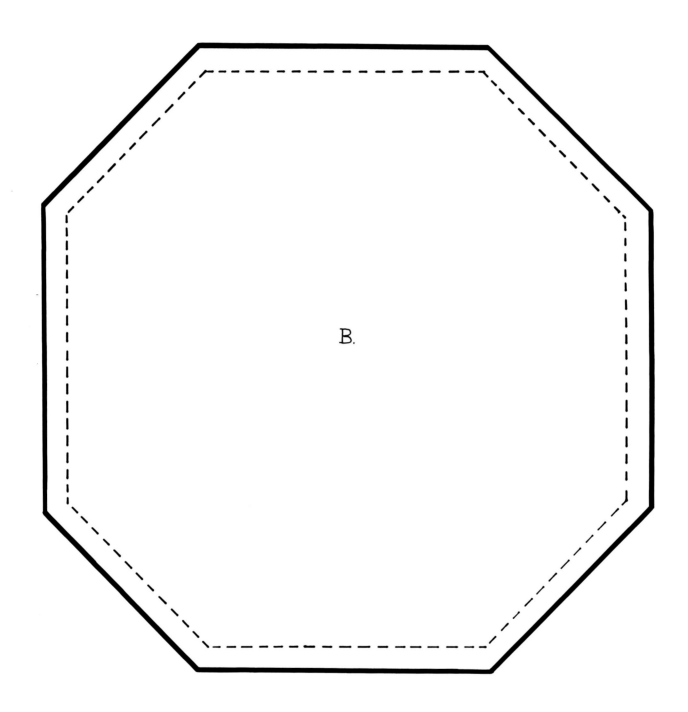

B.

Star of My Heart wall quilt template.
(Seam allowance included)

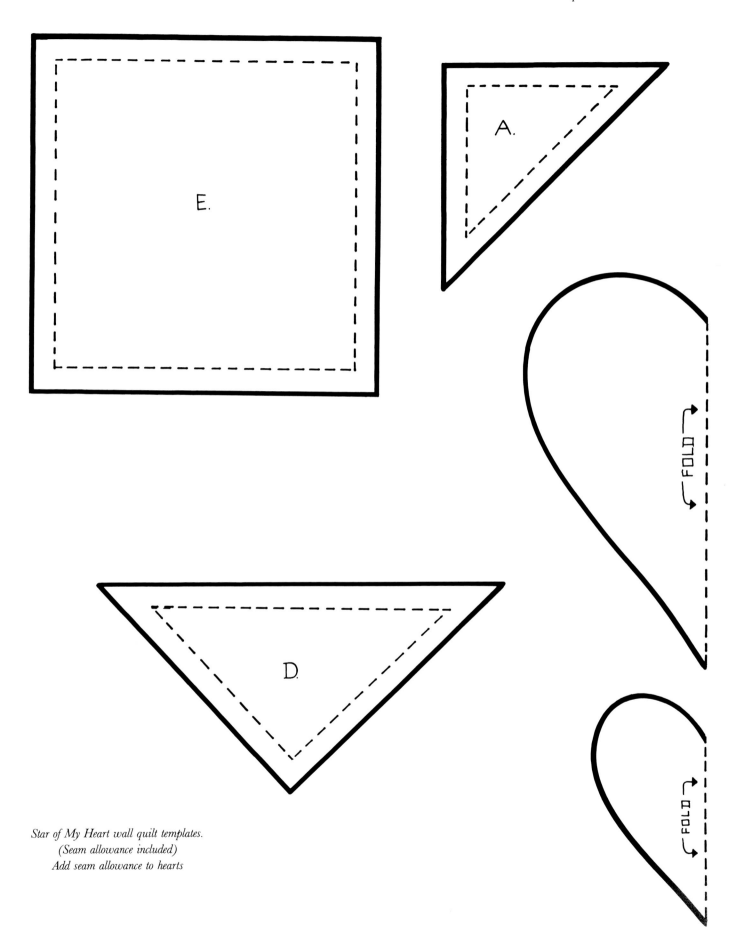

E.

A.

FOLD

D.

FOLD

Star of My Heart wall quilt templates.
(Seam allowance included)
Add seam allowance to hearts

place in each square, the measurements below correspond. You need the light and dark contrast on the "Star Block" corner. The lighter fabric in the "Snowball Block" helps to create contrast and movement.

1¾ yd. backing
1¾ yd. 3 oz. bonded batting
½ yd. black border and binding
¼ yd. green border fabric
For each Snowball block:
¾ yd. center Piece B
⅓ yd. corners Piece A
6" hearts (small)
For each Star block:
⅓ yd. center
⅓ yd. star points Piece A
½ yd. background Piece D
¼ yd. half-square corner (light) Piece A
¼ yd. half-square corner (dark) Piece A
½ yd. fabric for larger hearts scraps for half-squares in border Piece A
thread to match

Instructions:

1. Following the "Star of My Heart" instructions, make twenty-three star blocks and twenty-two snowball blocks. Be sure you use the wall quilt templates, not the sampler quilt templates. The corner half-squares can be made more quickly using the method described in "Piecing" in Part Five. Whenever possible, I streamline the cutting by stacking.

2. Arrange the blocks. Stitch them together in rows, then attach the rows to each other. Press.

3. First border (black):
Cut two 1¼" x 30½"—top and bottom
Cut two 1¼" x 54½"—sides
Add the top and bottom borders. Press. Add side borders, and press.

4. Pieced border: Cut eighty half-squares to form forty full squares, using template A. Look at Photo 4 for the arranging sequence. The half-squares will be 1½"-square finished.
Cut two 1½" x 18" strips—top and bottom
Cut two 1½" x 39½"—sides
Attach four of the split squares to each end of the top and bottom border. Press.
Stitch to the top and bottom of the quilt. Press. Add six of the split squares to each end of the side borders. Press.

5. Third border (black again):
Cut two 1¾" x 36"—top and bottom
Cut two 1¾" x 60½"—sides

Add top and bottom borders. Press. Then add the side borders, and press.

6. This quilt is machine quilted where the blocks are stitched to each other. Then hand quilting is done on the hearts. No marking for quilting was necessary. If you choose another theme for quilting, mark the quilting lines. Layer the quilt, then machine or hand quilt.

7. Enough seam allowance was allowed so the last border turns to the back ½", then half of that turns under and is hand stitched in place. This leaves a ¾" border on the front.

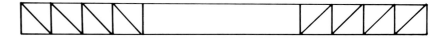

Border

They will be ¾" finished (1½" wide with both rows). Read the instructions in "Piecing" in Part Five for help in making the grid. Stitch two rows together that measure 8".

3. Stitch A to B to C to D to E. Press seams. Stitch around the heart shape ¼" from the raw edge. Clip at the center.

4. Hand appliqué the heart to the 8½" x 8½" square.

11. HEART STRIPS

The "Heart Strips" block has become one of my favorites. It has the curved feeling of hearts, but the checked insert creates wonderful design possibilities when placed with other hearts. See the quilt in Photo 11. It has an updated '50s look and fits perfectly in my daughter's bedroom. I was so taken with the design that I made myself a sweatshirt, adding ribbons, of course.

The shapes drawn in the top section have been quilted in the sampler, but could be appliquéd in place.

Materials needed:
1½" x 8" fabric for Piece A
2" x 8" fabric for Piece B
½" x 8" fabric for Piece C
1¼" x 45" fabric for Piece D
  (first color)
1¼" x 45" fabric for Piece D
  (second color)
2¾" x 4½" fabric for Piece E
8½" x 8½" fabric for background
thread to match

Instructions:
1. Cut out Pieces A, B, C, and E. Be sure to add ¼" seam allowance.

2. To make the grid (the D pieces), cut the strips 1¼" wide.

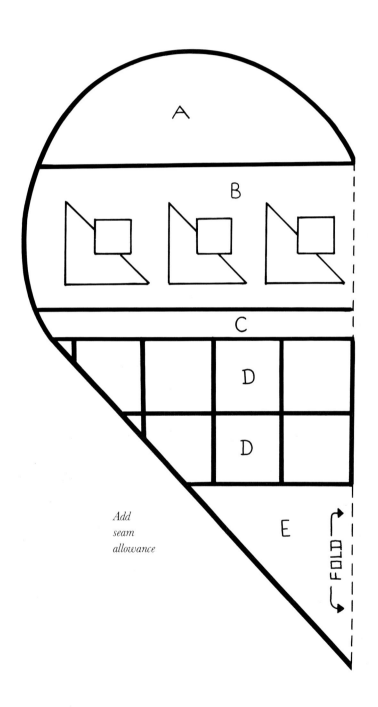

11A. Heart Strips Quilt
Finished size 22¾" x 22¾"
(Photo 11)

Four "Heart Strips" are pieced and stitched together to form checkerboard hearts. As the four blocks join together, they create a new design where the checkerboard becomes dominant and the heart shape secondary. The heart tops appear as petals. This quilt has a '50s feel to it, especially when done in solid bright colors.

Materials needed:
2¼ yds. white fabric
½ yd. turquoise fabric
½ yd. hot pink fabric
¼ yd. black fabric
¼ yd. light pink fabric
¼ yd. light turquoise fabric
¾ yd. 3 oz. bonded batting
thread to match

Instructions:
Cut out the following pieces:
white:
1 - 18¼" x 18¼"
5 - 1" x 44"
4 - 3½" x 24"
4 - 1½" x 24"
black:
5 - 1" x 44"
turquoise:
2 - 2½" x 44"
hot pink:
2 - 2½" x 44"
light turquoise:
1 - 1" x 44"
light pink:
1 - 1" x 44"
Heart piecing fabrics: Use the "Heart Strips" pattern and add ¼" seam allowance to the edges.

1. Using the "Heart Strips" instructions, cut and piece the four hearts. Press. When making the checkerboard, stitch all the black and white strips together. Some will be used for the border.

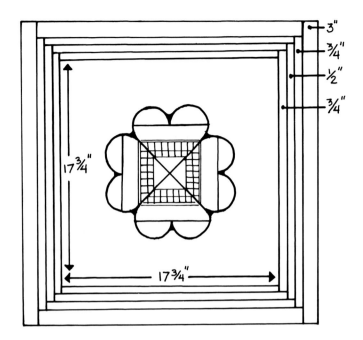

2. Topstitch ¼" from the edge around the four hearts.

3. Stitch two hearts together down the side. Stitch the other two together. Press open the seam allowance.

4. Join the two heart sections to form the four-heart design. Press.

5. Place the four hearts on the 18¼" x 18¼" white fabric. Hand appliqué in place.

6. Stitch the turquoise and hot pink 2½"-wide strips together. Press. Cut across seams 1¼" wide.

7. Add strips around the border, starting with turquoise. Eventually, you will trim off the hot pink and it becomes a square. Press.

8. Add the black-and-white checked border. Press. Then add the last turquoise and hot pink border.

9. Add white border, mitering the corners. See "The Finishing Touch" in Part Five for further instructions.

10. The quilt in Photo 11 is machine quilted. The heart shapes were repeated. Layer the quilt, then quilt it.

11B. Heart Strips Sweatshirt
(Photo 11)

"Heart Strips" appears as an appliqué on this sweatshirt. Most of the hearts in this book can be adapted to sweatshirt decorations, making an ordinary piece of clothing something special.

Materials needed:
1 prewashed sweatshirt
1 "Heart Strips" heart
Wonder-Under Fusible Web®
ribbons (optional)
thread to match

Instructions:
1. Using the "Heart Strips" instructions, construct one heart.
2. Add Wonder-Under to the back of the heart and fuse to a prewashed sweatshirt.
3. Machine appliqué in place.
4. Ribbons may be added for embellishment.

11C. Sewing Caddy
(Photo 6)

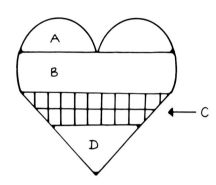

Marina dreamed up this idea, and I executed it. This caddy can lay on a table or be mounted on a wall.

Materials needed:
⅛ yd. fabric for Pieces A, B, and D
2½″ x 45″ Piece C (color 1)
2½″ x 45″ Piece C (color 2)
⅓ yd. backing
½ lb. Polyfil®
½ yd. ½″-wide elastic
1 yd. each of two colors of ribbon ⅜″-wide
thread to match

Instructions:

1. Use the "Heart Strips" pattern for the hearts, adding ¼″ seam allowance.

2. Cut four pieces of A, B, and D.

3. Follow piecing instructions in Part Five. Make the grid (the C pieces).

4. Sew A and B together. Sew C and D together.

5. Cut four linings for Sections C and D. Place the right side of lining to the right side of each heart on four hearts. Stitch across the top. Turn to the right side, and press.

6. Using the remaining four heart linings, stitch them to Sections A-B.

7. Place finished Sections C-D on top of A-B, matching side seams. Baste the side seams.

8. Cut out four backings for the hearts. Place the lining on each heart and stitch around the edge, leaving a 3″ opening on the side. Clip curves. Turn to the right side. Stuff with Polyfil. Whipstitch opening closed.

9. Using lining fabric, cut a strip 1¾″ x 36″. Make a casing for the elastic. Insert the elastic. The fabric will gather up.

10. Pull the elastic around a spool of thread you would put in the caddy. Place a pin where the elastic meets. Allow ¼″ at each end.

11. Zigzag stitch the elastic ends together. Make four of these, one for each corner.

12. Hand tack the hearts together. Insert elastic in corners, hand tacking in place.

13. Embellish with ribbon bows.

12. AT HOME WITH HEARTS

This is the final block in our sampler quilt and sums up our feelings about hearts. Both of our homes are brimming with hearts.

Blue-and-white checkerboards have such a clean look that they were chosen for the grid and house. The border was left off the sampler block.

Materials needed:
8½" x 8½" square background fabric
5½" x 6" for heart
1" x 45" color 1 for grid
1" x 45" color 2 for grid
scraps for house and hearts
thread to match

Instructions:
1. Cut an 8½" x 8½" square. Make templates. Cut the remaining pieces, adding ¼" seam allowance.
2. To make the grid, follow piecing instructions in Part Five. Make the grid 6" x 2½".
3. Place the grid on the 8½" x 8½" background. Hand appliqué.
4. Using the freezer paper appliqué method, appliqué all other pieces in place.

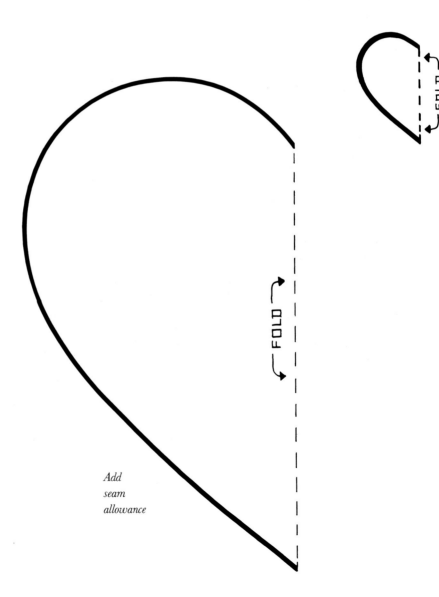

FOLD

FOLD

Add seam allowance

12A. Framed Recipe Holder
(Photo 8)

This recipe holder is not only decorative but functional. Place it on your kitchen counter. The plastic pocket keeps a 3″ x 5″ recipe card clean and easily seen when you cook.

Materials needed:
10″ x 12″ base fabric
¼ yd. Wonder-Under Fusible Web®
fabric scraps
3½″ x 5½″ mediumweight clear plastic
3½″ x 5½″ fabric
⅔ yd. ⅜″-wide lace
two ribbon roses
8″ x 10″ needlework foam mounting board
picture frame (8″ x 10″ opening— select the type that has a back prop)
tracing paper
tubed fabric pens (optional)
strapping tape
thread to match

Instructions:
1. Using the ''At Home with Hearts'' instructions, trace the house heart motif pieces. Apply Wonder-Under to your chosen fabrics, and cut out the pattern pieces. The corner areas may be checkered or left in a solid piece.

2. For a checkered look, cut 30 ½″ x ½″ squares (18 dark and 12 light color). Cut two 2¾″ x 2¾″ triangles. Lay out the squares in a light/dark pattern. Trim excess off the side that will join the large heart. Fuse.

3. Lay all pattern pieces on base fabric in this order: checkered triangles, large heart, heart point triangle, house, door, and house heart. Adjust the design so that it is centered; there should be 5¼″

from the tip of the large heart to the bottom of the base fabric. Fuse. Cut a 3½″ x 5½″ piece of fabric. Fuse directly below the heart design, lining up edges.

4. Cut a 3½″ x 5½″ piece of clear plastic. Place directly over the fused design and hand stitch ⅛″ from the edge of the rectangle on three sides, leaving the top open.

5. Optional: Using tubed fabric pens, trace over the edges of the design as desired. Refer to Photo 8 for lace placement. Glue.

6. Mount on foam board following manufacturer's instructions. Place in frame.

12B. At Home with Hearts Chair Cushion
(Photo 4)

A chair cushion can be decorative as well as functional. The house design just seemed to fit the mood of the wall quilt in Photo 4. Machine appliqué was used on the house and small hearts.

Materials needed:
⅝ yd. Fabric #1 (dark green stripe print—behind house)
¼ yd. Fabric #2 (dark green floral print—heart)
⅔ yd. Fabric #3 (red print—house front border)
12″ x 13″ Fabric #4 (green plaid— roof)
10″ x 10″ Fabric #5 (medium-weight cream solid—heart)
5″ x 5″ Fabric #6 (red print— house)
3″ x 4″ Fabric #7 (red/cream plaid—house)
3½″ x 7″ Fabric #8 (light and dark green print—ground)
2″ x 3″ Fabric #9 (green solid— door)
3″ x 10″ Fabric #10 (red print)
½ yd. Thermolam®

½ yd. 3 oz. batting
15″ x 15″ piece 1¼″-thick foam rubber
1 pkg. (or 25″) maxi-piping, cream-colored
1½ yds. ⅜″ cording
1 pkg. (4 yds.) single-fold narrow bias tape, red
thread to match

Instructions:
1. Enlarge the ''At Home with Hearts'' design (use a copy machine) until the large heart shape is 7″ tall.
Cushion Back:
Cut:
Fabric #1 —4½″ x 15½″ piece (heart base)
two 13″ x 14″ x 16½″ pieces (seat cushion; see diagram)
Fabric #2 —two 2¾″ x 45″ strips (ruffle)
one heart on house
Fabric #3 —three 8″ x 8″ pieces (for bias strip)
two 1½″ x 11½″ strips (border)
two 1½″ x 15″ strips (border)
13½″ x 15″ piece (cushion back)
Fabric #4 —10″ x 11½″ piece (cushion front)
one of roof
Fabric #5 —3½″ x 11½″ piece (cushion border)
one of large heart
Fabric #6 —one of left-hand side of house
Fabric #7 —one of right-hand side of house
Fabric #8 —one of ground
Fabric #9 —one of door
Fabric #10—four hearts on border
Cut the foam rubber (see diagram), rounding the back corners slightly or cut the foam to fit your chair.

2. Fuse appliqué pieces to larger heart. Machine appliqué. The bottom of the house need not be

appliquéd. Lay the ground down, edges even with the bottom of the house, and stitch. Flip to right side up, and baste it to the bottom of the heart. Fuse the small hearts to the cushion border, and machine appliqué.

3. Fold the heart base in half crosswise, right sides together, and stitch the ends. Press open the seam allowance. Turn. Press flat, with seam in center back. Mark the center of the base, then mark the center of the border. Lay the right sides together, matching centers, and pin together. Lay the border on the cushion front, right sides together, with the heart base sandwiched between. Stitch through all layers. Press the seam allowance toward the border. Baste the top of the heart base to the cushion front.

4. Sew the piping to the heart, starting and ending ¼″ from the top V of the heart. Clip the piping seam allowance and pivot at the bottom V of the heart. Then clip the top V. Turn the seam allowance to the back of the heart and press. Lay the heart in position over the base. Pin. Stitch in ditch around piping.

5. Sew the 11½″ border strips to the top and bottom edges of the cushion front. Press seam toward border. Sew the 15″ border strips to sides. Press seam toward border.

6. Lay the cushion front on the batting and cut to fit. Do the same with the Thermolam. Set aside.

7. Join the ends of the ruffle strips. Cut to measure 84½″. Sew ends, forming a tube, and narrow hem one edge. Divide in fourths and mark. Gather stitch between marks. Divide the cushion front edge in fourths and mark. Match marks and pull gathers to fit. Baste around sides.

8. Fold the red bias tape in half lengthwise and stitch it close to the edge. Cut into twelve 12″ tie pieces. Baste two tie pieces to each corner of the cushion front, raw edges even. Tie a knot on the end of each tie. Set aside the remaining four ties for the seat cushion.

9. Lay the cushion top on the batting, then on the Thermolam. Place the cushion back on the cushion top, right sides together, and pin. Stitch, leaving opening. Turn.

Cushion Seat:

1. Sew bias strip with three 8″ x 8″ pieces of Fabric #3. Cut in 1½″-wide strips and piece to measure 60″.

2. Cut Thermolam piece to fit seat. Baste to wrong side of seat.

3. Sew cording to the seat front, overlapping at center back. Clip the bias strip edge at curves and corners. Sew two ties to each back corner, raw edges even. Tie knots on tie ends.

4. Place seat back on top, right sides together, and stitch, leaving back side open. Turn, then press. Insert the foam rubber. Whipstitch the opening closed.

12C. Towel Topper
(Photo 8)

"At Home with Hearts" is the perfect appliqué design for the kitchen towel topper. Velcro holds the tab together at the top. A heart border was added to the bottom of the towel.

Materials needed:
¼ yd. white fabric for heart
⅛ yd. border and bottom of heart design (blue check)
scrap—house (light rose print)
scrap—house (cream print)
scrap—roof (blue print)
⅛ yd. for hearts (dark rose print)
⅛ yd. for ground (dark green solid)
¼ yd. binding (dark rose solid)
3″ x 9″ rose plaid fabric
one rose-colored hand towel
¼ yd. Thermolam®
½ yd. ⅛″ cording
1″ piece Velcro
Wonder-Under Fusible Web®
thread to match

Instructions:
Use the "At Home with Hearts" pattern. Add ⅜″ around the outside edge of the heart. Locate two small dots on side of heart where the towel will connect.

1. Cut fabric:
white:
two hearts
1″ x width of towel + 2″ for border
blue check:
3¾″ x 12½″ piece (towel band)
2½″ x width of towel + 2″ (towel border)
light rose print:
one piece house side with door
cream:
one piece house front
blue print:
one piece roof
dark rose print:
one piece heart, one piece door, eight border hearts
dark green solid:
ground 1⅝″ x width of towel + 2″ (strip #2)

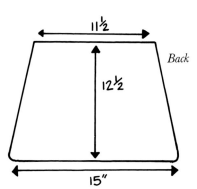

11½
12½
15″
Back

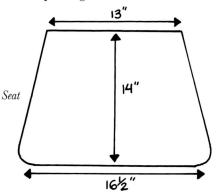

13″
14″
16½″
Seat

dark rose solid:
two 8″ squares
rose plaid:
2¾″ x 8½″ piece (strap) (these could be the same print)
Thermolam:
two hearts, one 3¾″ x 5¾″ (for band)
Cut the towel to measure 15″ in length.

2. Fuse appliqué pieces to one heart. Machine appliqué. The bottom of the house need not be appliquéd. Lay the ground fabric over the bottom of the appliqué, and stitch. Flip right side up and baste to the bottom of the heart.

3. Make a bias strip from two 8″ squares of rose solid. Cut the strip to 1″ x 18½″. Fold it crosswise, then stitch across the ends. Cut an 18″ length of cording. Encase the cording in bias strip, using the zipper foot on your machine. Lay two Thermolam pieces under the heart top, and baste around their edges. Baste the covered cording to the heart top. Place the remaining heart top and stitch

between the two small dots (using your zipper foot to get close to the cording), leaving the bottom of the heart open. Turn right side out.

4. Border: Press the green and white strips in half lengthwise. Lay them on the long edge of the border piece (green behind white), then sew them to the border piece, stitching through both strips. Press seam allowance towards band. Fuse eight hearts to the border and appliqué. Sew the border to the towel, 2″ up from the towel's bottom edge. Stitch the bottom of the border first (it will extend 1″ beyond each side of the towel), then flip the border up and stitch in the ditch along the white strip. Whipstitch the ends of the border to the towel's back side.

5. Gather the towel's top edge and draw it up to 6″. Fold towel band piece in half crosswise, and stitch the ends. With seam to back side of towel, sandwich gathered edge of towel inside of band, top edges even. Pin. Lay band on top of the Thermolam piece, with the

seam side of the band facing up. Stitch ½″ from edge, through all thicknesses. Turn band to right side out. Stitch across the top edge.

6. Insert the top of the towel band into the heart piece, and pin in place. Stitch in the ditch on the bottom half of the heart, along the cording (keeping heart facing free from stitching), tucking seam allowance to inside of heart as you stitch. Turn under the edge of the heart facing, and whipstitch to the back of the towel band.

7. Strap: Fold strap piece lengthwise, right sides together. Lay Thermolam under the strap piece and stitch along both the edge and the end. Clip corner, turn, and press. Sew one Velcro half ¼″ from the raw edge of the strap. Sew the other half to the opposite end, same side, of the strap. Whipstitch the end of the strap to the heart facing, turning under the raw edge. Tack at the top of the heart facing.

13. HEART EXTRACTIONS

For all those projects that take a single heart and repeat it, we have reserved this chapter. Other heart shapes are also explored.

13A. Pieced Heart Design

This heart shape appears in the border on the heartworks sample (front cover). The same shape is machine appliquéd on the tummy of the bear garland. Here's a place to let your imagination go.

To piece this shape, cut two of A, B, and C, adding ¼ " seam allowance and remembering there will be a seam where the dotted line appears. Piece A to B and B to C, then press. Repeat for the other side of the heart. (Remember this is a mirror image if you're working with fabric with a right and wrong side.) Join the two sides, and press the seam. This design can easily be enlarged, perhaps into an entire quilt.

13B. Soft at Heart Quilt
Finished size 19" x 26"
(Photo 6)

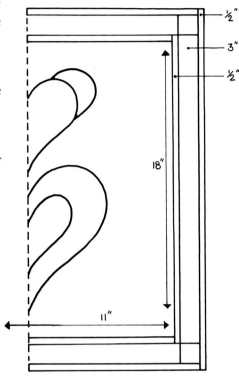

Russian folk art inspired this project. The black print fabric suggested colors for the quilt. Battenburg lace was tea-dyed to blend with the fabrics.

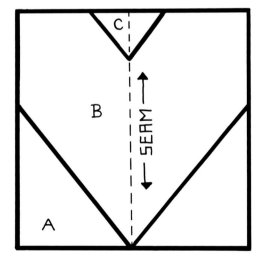

Add seam allowance

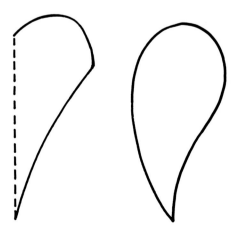

Materials needed:
1 yd. print fabric
⅓ yd. center background fabric
¼ yd. narrow border fabric
⅓ yd. wide border fabric
⅛ yd. bright accent fabric
1½ yd. lace
½ yd. 3 oz. bonded batting
freezer paper for appliqué
thread to match

Instructions:
1. To make patterns for the hearts in the center, follow the diagram.
large heart:
Cut two pieces of print fabric (finished size 10½" tall, 10" wide).
corners:
Cut four pieces 3½" x 3½". Using the small heart, cut eight heart corners.
backing:
Cut a piece of backing 20" x 27".

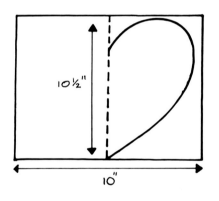

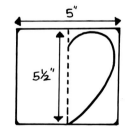

small heart:
Cut four of wide border fabric (finished size 5½" tall, 5" wide).
wide borders:
Cut two pieces 3½" x 12½", and two 3½" x 19½".

Cut narrow borders: five 1" x 44"
Cut center background: 12" x 19"
Cut batting: 20" x 27"

2. Following the patterns, cut 14 centers from the bright accent fabric. Add ¼" seam allowance. Cut 14 freezer paper shapes the exact size. Press the freezer paper to the fabric. Cut 28 side pieces from the narrow border fabric. Add seam allowance. Cut 14 freezer paper side pieces, then turn the pattern over and cut 14 more. This creates the mirror image pieces. Press the freezer paper to the fabric.

3. To make the hearts and heart corner sections in the center panel, follow the instructions on ''Dimensional Hearts'' in Part Five.

4. Position hearts on background. Add appliqué using the freezer paper appliqué method.

5. To position the lace, you may need to gather it slightly at the corners so it will curve. Tack it to the back of the heart. Hand stitch the dimensional hearts in place.

6. Add narrow borders to center panels. Press.

7. Add wide border at top and bottom. Press.

8. Stitch corners to the ends of the side borders. Press. Attach to the side of the quilt. Press.

9. Add final narrow border.

10. Add final appliqués on borders.

11. Layer the quilt. This quilt is machine quilted at each seam line.

12. Trim excess batting and backing to within ⅓" of the raw edge of the final border. Turn under edge of binding ¼" and pull to the back of the quilt. Hand stitch in place.

13C. Hearts in Friendship Pillow
Finished size 13½" x 13½"
(Photo 7)

Hearts were cut freehand to form this bouquet of friendship. Quilting is also done freehand in a spontaneous mood to emphasize the design. Ribbons trail from each heart and are gathered together with a large bow.

This design is so spontaneous, it could easily become rectangular or vertical as well. The hearts are backed with freezer paper and appliquéd in place. The hearts are 3" finished and cut freehand, then placed on a 13½" x 13½" background. Small 1½" hearts were sewn, stuffed, and placed in the corners attached to ribbon scraps.

Materials needed:
three 13½" x 13½" squares for front and back of pillow
scraps of seven fabrics for the hearts
2 yds. ⅛"-wide ribbon for stems
⅝ yd. ⅞"-wide ribbon for bow
13½" x 13½" 3 oz. bonded batting
1 lb. Polyfil®
freezer paper for heart appliqué
embroidery floss
thread to match

Instructions:

1. Cut seven hearts approximately 3¼" x 3¼" out of freezer paper. Press the freezer paper, waxed side down, to seven different fabrics. Cut out heart shapes ¼" beyond the edge of the freezer paper.

2. Place them on one of the 13½" squares. Place a piece of ribbon at the base of each. Hand appliqué.

3. Place the batting and backing under the top. Baste the sections together with large hand stitches. Hand quilt inside each heart design ¼" from the edge. Add hand quilting around the outside edges of the hearts.

4. Pull the ribbons together like a bouquet. Tack in place.

5. Tie a bow out of the ⅞"-wide ribbon. Tack at the center knot. Add French knots to hold the tails of the bow in place (see "Embellishments" in Part Five).

6. Add the backing to the pillow, and stuff.

13D. Hearts and Flowers Quilt

by Nadine Thompson
Finished size 22" x 26"
(Photo 1)

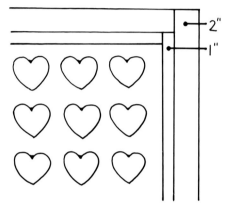

Nadine's precious floral quilt came to my attention when I was visiting "Going to Pieces," a quilt shop in Pleasanton, California. She said she "carefully cut the appliqué hearts using the best portions of the flower prints." As you can see from Photo 1, this careful planning paid off in creating a stunning floral heart design.

Materials needed:

½ yd. background fabric for hearts
¼ yd. first border fabric
½ yd. second border fabric
⅛ yd. binding
⅞ yd. backing
⅞ yd. fleece
5" scraps for each heart, or ⅛ yd. if you must purchase fabric
freezer paper for heart appliqué
thread to match

Instructions:

1. Cut background piece 16½" x 20½". Then cut:
first border:
2 strips—1½" x 16½"
2 strips—1½" x 22½"
second border:
2 strips—2½" x 18½"
2 strips—2½" x 26½"

Seam allowance included

binding:
2 strips—2" x 44"
backing and fleece:
18" x 22"

2. Using the actual size template, cut 20 hearts from freezer paper. Press the waxy side of the paper to the wrong side of the heart fabric. Cut fabric a scant ¼" beyond freezer paper.

3. Center hearts on the background fabric, remembering there is a ¼" seam allowance allowed around the edges. Pin in place.

4. Appliqué by hand, using the freezer paper method.

5. Add the top and bottom first borders. Press. Add first side borders.

6. Add second borders in the same sequence as Step 5. Press.

7. Layer the quilt, and machine or hand quilt it.

8. Add binding.

13E. Band Boxes
(Photos 5 and 8)

Band boxes come in six sizes, from tiny to large, so your imagination can run wild! Suzy Lawson, owner of Amity Publications, has teamed with Bev Soasey to design the boxes and patterns. Band boxes can hold all kinds of treasures, from sewing tools to jewelry, or even a special gift.

On both boxes shown here, I have followed the instructions given by Amity; then I embellished the boxes. Materials needed are listed in the Amity pattern.

The "Victorian Hearts" box uses box size C. In the top, I cut freehand three sizes of hearts from muslin, the largest 3" high, the

smallest 1¾" high. Using the crazy patch method of piecing, I made three hearts, then did the fourth heart in a solid color. The largest is trimmed with heart lace and narrow rat-tail cord. Ribbon loops are formed, stitched together, and put behind the large heart. Then the smaller hearts are stacked up against each other. Buttons flow randomly from the hearts.

"At Home with Hearts" uses box size D. The pattern is fused to the lid using Wonder-Under®. The lid side is trimmed with bows. To form the bows, shape them and put tacky glue between the layers, then hold them with a clothspin. Once the glue dries, put more glue on the bow back and clothespin each one to the box until dry.

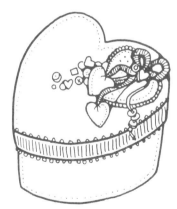

13F. Freehand Hearts Quilt
by Nancy Taylor
Finished size 31" x 31"
(Photo 3)

Nancy Taylor designed "Freehand Hearts" and added a multitude of borders to create this delightful quilt.

She has cut all the hearts freehand to give a folk art feeling. Her choice of colors is reminiscent of southwest moods. In choosing your colors, note where Nancy has used bright colors and the quieter dark colors. The use of the brights is what makes this quilt sing.

Materials needed:
Scraps can be used for most of this quilt, so inch measurements are given.
Scraps for squares and hearts—
   hearts are cut 5¼"
A Border—black—5" x 44"
B Border—stripe—6" x 44"
C Border—burgundy pin stripe—
   7" x 44"
D Border—black—6" x 44"
E Border—magenta pin dot—
   4" x 44"
F Border—periwinkle floral—
   4" x 44"
G Border—black—4" x 44"
H Border—black—6" x 44"
32" x 32" backing
32" x 32" 3 oz. bonded batting
thread to match

Instructions:

1. Cut 16 5¼" x 5¼" squares. Cut 16 hearts freely from fabric scraps. Don't worry; they aren't supposed to be exactly alike.

borders:
A—2 - 1⅛" strips
B—2 - 1¾" strips
C—2 - 2½" strips
D—2 - 1½" strips
E—3 - ¾" strips
F—4 - ⅞" strips
G—4 - ⅞" strips
H—4 - 1½" strips

2. Hand appliqué the heart in each square.

3. Join the squares, sewing four squares across, then sewing those rows of blocks together.

4. There are several—many!—borders to this unique quilt, each added in the same manner; first attach the top and bottom border pieces, then the side pieces.

5. Layer the quilt. Then machine or hand quilt it.

13G. Patriotic Pillow
(Photo 2)

The patriotic pillow just crept into the scene once "Piece of My Heart" bear was finished. Stuffed stars hang from the top edge of the pillow. The heart is machine appliquéd, then topstitched in white.

Materials needed:
7" x 7" piece of red and white star print
5" x 5" piece of blue and white star print
⅛ yd. each of six different "patriotic" prints
⅛ yd. of gold solid (for stars)
⅜ yd. of cream print (for pillow back)
1⅔ yd. ⅛" cording
1 pkg. single-fold wide bias tape, cream-colored (or 60")

1 pkg. double-fold narrow bias tape, cream-colored (or 27")
1 lb. Polyfil®
white topstitching thread
thread to match

Instructions:
1. Cut:
one 6½" x 6½" piece of red star print
one heart shape of blue star print
three 2½" x 11½" strips of patriotic prints
three 2½" x 17½" strips of patriotic prints
one 12½" x 17½" piece of pillow back print
four star shapes of gold solid

2. Fuse the heart shape to the red square, and machine appliqué. Stitch around the heart, just inside the machine appliqué stitching, with topstitching thread. Stitch slowly and carefully, "walking" the needle with the hand wheel around curves. Pull bobbin threads

in back to draw topstitching thread to the back, and knot.

3. Sew six strips together, first three 11½", then three 17½", with the right side ends even. Press.

4. Unfold double-fold bias tape, and press it flat. Cover ⅛" cording with bias tape, using the zipper foot on your sewing machine. Baste cording to the right and bottom sides of the square, holding the square fabric tight as you stitch. Turn the piece over and stitch again, getting stitching a little closer to the cording. Press seam allowance toward square. Lay the square on the pillow top, having seam allowances overlap. Pin. Change machine thread to red, and stitch in the ditch around the cording.

5. Cut one 5½" and one 7½" length of double-fold bias tape. Unfold and press it flat. Fold bias tape in half lengthwise over a piece of narrow ribbon or string. Stitch across the end, through ribbon, and along edge, being sure not to catch ribbon in stitching. Clip corner and pull the ribbon to turn right side out. Clip off ribbon. Sew tie to a star piece, raw edges even.

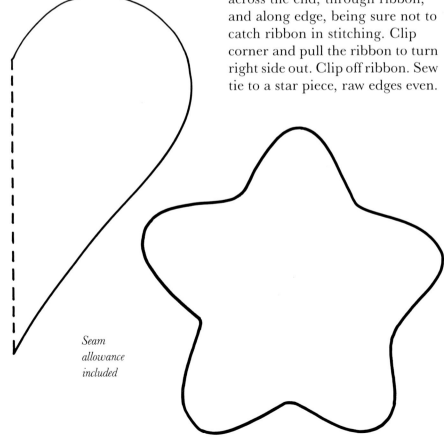

Seam allowance included

Lay another star on top and stitch around, leaving opening. Clip edges and turn. Press and stuff tightly. Whipstitch closed. Repeat with the other tie and star. Sew the tie ends to the top left corner of the pillow top, raw edges even.

6. Cover ⅛" cording with single-fold bias tape (pressed flat). Trim tape to ¼" from the stitching. Sew cording to the pillow top, over-lapping ends at the top left corner. Round corners slightly, clipping the edge of the bias tape as you round corner.

7. Lay pillow top and back, right sides together, and pin. Stitch, leaving opening. Turn the pillow over and restitch, to get closer to cording. Turn and press. Stuff, then whipstitch closed.

13H. Tablecloth
(Photo 1)

Our tablecloth is pulled up at four corners and tied with ribbons and tiny stuffed hearts. To make a round cloth, first measure the table top and two side drops. You will need to cut a circle this measurement. I used a 45" circle. The edge of the circle can be machine hemmed, or cording can be added like ours.

Pull up corners the desired amount. It's best to put the cloth on the table and then pin up the corners. Make tiny pleats or gathers and secure by hand. Add ribbons or cloth bows with stuffed hearts.

Materials needed:
1¼ yd. fabric for tablecloth
½ yd. contrasting fabric for piping
6 yds. ⅛" cording
⅛ yd. each of four different fabrics for hearts
3 yds. ¼"-wide ribbon

¼ lb. Polyfil®
thread to match

Instructions:
1. Cut a circle from the table-cloth fabric.

2. Cut bias strip 1" wide from the contrast fabric. Cut enough to make six yards. Follow instructions in Part Five to make cording.

3. Add cording around the edge of the tablecloth.

4. Fold the tablecloth into four sections. Put a pin at each one. To form the corners, make six ¼" folds and stitch them together.

5. Cut eight hearts approximately 2" x 2". Cut 16 hearts approximately 1½" x 1½".

6. Stitch the hearts like little pillows. Stuff with Polyfil. Close the opening.

7. Cut four ribbons 4" long. Cut eight ribbons 3½" long. Cut four ribbons 3" long. Tack a ribbon to a heart making a loop at the top.

8. Put one ribbon of each length together and tack at each corner.

13I. Watermelon Slippers
(Photo 11)

Purchase a pair of slippers, then decorate them with your favorite appliqué. Here the bottom half of the heart has become a watermelon.

Materials needed:
one pair slip-on slippers
¼ yd. pink print
5½" x 18" white fabric

6" x 8" scrap red print
⅛ yd. green fabric
5½" x 12" 3 oz. bonded batting
1 pkg. red pin-dot bias tape
⅞ yd. ⅛" cording
⅔ yd. 1⁄16"-wide pink ribbon
twelve black 6mm half-round beads
Wonder-Under Fusible Web®
felt-tipped pen
glue gun
thread to match

Instructions:
1. Make a pattern for the slipper band. Lay a piece of scrap fabric (muslin) over the band of the slipper, then with the felt-tipped pen, mark the edges of the band onto the fabric. Add ½" to all sides.

2. Cut:
pink print—four of slipper band (two band, two lining)
white fabric—two of Piece A; two of Piece B
red print—two of Piece C
green print—two of Piece D (use Wonder-Under); two 1¾" x 12½" strips (for ruffle)
batting—two of Piece A

3. Fold ruffle strips in half lengthwise. Stitch across the ends. Turn and press. Gather the long edge to fit width of the top edge of the slipper. Center ruffle on top edge of the slipper band, raw edges even, and baste. Lay lining on top, right sides together, and stitch. Turn, then press. Baste around the remaining sides of slipper band.

4. Place slipper band on the slipper. Line up ruffled edge, and pin. Turn opposite edge under to fit, and pin. Turn sides under and hand stitch to the slipper, going through to the inside of the slipper.

5. Watermelon heart: Fuse Piece D to Piece C. Machine appliqué the top edge with white thread. Sew Piece C to Piece B, right sides together, and press the seam toward

B. Cut bias tape in two 15″ lengths. Cover cording with bias strips. Sew to the heart pieces, starting and ending by overlapping cording at the bottom point of heart. Lay the heart pieces on batting. Top with Piece A and pin. Stitch around the heart, close to cording, leaving an opening on the side. Turn, and whipstitch the opening closed. Press lightly. Cut the ribbon length in half, then make two bows. Center the heart on the slipper band and sew bow to the top of the heart; stitching through the slipper. Tack the heart to the slipper band at the bottom and sides, allowing the heart to flare out slightly on the sides. Glue black beads to the heart with your glue gun.

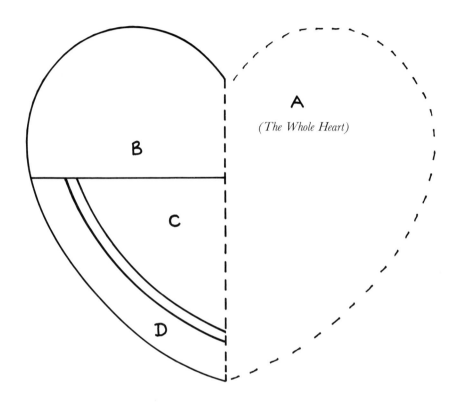

A

(The Whole Heart)

B

C

D

FIVE
Heart to Heart Basics

Tools and Tricks of the Trade

Just like a carpenter, you'll need to keep your quilting tools in good repair if you want accurate measurements and a flat piece of work. My scissors are sharpened often, and I keep a backup pair just in case. My sewing machine is maintained regularly, and I have the tension adjusted twice a year. Over the years, I have found it is definitely worth it to purchase quality tools, and to keep them in excellent repair.

Rotary Cutter, Mat, Ruler, and Glue Sticks

The first time I saw a rotary cutter, I thought it was just a flashy gimmick. Well, I was totally wrong. These tools have made patchwork faster and very accurate. A large rotary cutter is the best choice for larger pieces, but for smaller pieces, keep a smaller cutter on hand. An 18″ x 24″ cutting mat should be sufficient for most projects.

Several quilting rulers are on the market. Be sure to select one with the standard measurements, plus markings for 45° and 60°. The quarter-inch markings should be clear and easy to read. At first, I used a 6″ x 24″ ruler, which I liked, but last year I purchased a 6″ x 12″

one and find it especially useful for small pieces. Now there's a 6″ square ruler available with a diagonal line from corner to corner and a ¼″ grid. I've found it very helpful for cutting squares and half-triangles.

Glue sticks are invaluable. I use them almost like an extra hand for holding down appliqué pieces before they're permanently secured.

Fabrics

You will be more successful using 100% cotton, higher quality fabrics. With the time you put into special projects, it's worth it to work on quality fabrics. They'll be more flexible as you work with smaller pieces, and they'll stand the test of time. After purchasing fabrics, wash and dry them first before using in any project. Soap helps to set the dyes. Some fabrics, especially dark ones, are often over-dyed. It may take several washings to get the extra dye out. Repeated use of a hot dryer is deadly to fabrics, as the heat breaks down the fibers. Tumble-dry using a lower heat setting, or line dry your fabrics.

I must share with you a story I overheard recently in my store. A

customer was at the counter debating how much yardage to buy, and she lamented, "I have so much fabric already. I just can't buy more." Another customer said, "But you know you have to *age* your fabric." Everyone in the store laughed. We were all relieved that our fabric stashes were okay since they were "aging."

Pattern Drafting

Full-size patterns are provided for the projects in this book. Those templates have a ¼″ seam allowance added. Just put your template material over the pattern, trace the shape, label it, and cut it out.

However, most of the heart shapes do *not* have a seam allowance added, since many of them are to be traced directly onto the fabric. Each block has general instructions that will tell you what to do.

All of the blocks can be enlarged or reduced. If you are unable to do that freehand, use a copy machine that can do it for you. The copy machine is an invaluable tool for making patterns; it can also be used to enlarge or reduce a pattern. It may take two or three copies to get the exact size but it's so fast. Many of our patterns just need to be ½″ or 1″ larger.

Whenever I have a heart shape to cut out, I fold the paper in half so it will be accurate. With practice, you'll be able to cut hearts out freehand. I keep all my paper hearts so I can use them in future projects.

Appliqué

Machine Appliqué

Machine appliqué can be a very effective technique on a project that will have a lot of use. I like the look of the firm stitching design. It adds another dimension to the project, almost like an outline. Your sewing machine needs to be in good working order if you are to achieve a professional look. In fact, I have my tension adjusted before big appliqué projects. An appliqué foot can be helpful if you have one.

When using cotton fabrics, a lightweight fusible interfacing can give the appliqué shape more body. Fuse the interfacing to the fabric, then cut out the heart. This shape can then be pinned in place or a glue stick can hold it down. I prefer the glue stick.

Wonder-Under Fusible Web® is also useful to fuse the appliqué fabric to the backing. Wonder-Under is a brand name for a web with a paper backing. The paper is pressed to the wrong side of the fabric. The shape is cut out and the paper peeled off. The shape is then pressed to the background fabric. This method produces a stiffer shape.

Another method involves straight stitching the appliqué, close to the raw edge, to the backing fabric before satin-stitching. This holds the appliqué shape secure while you satin-stitch. You can use a narrow satin-stitch. Test the stitch

width before you begin; and adapt it to the scale of the project. Adjust your stitch so that the needle enters just beyond the raw edge, then goes into the shape.

As you approach the inside V of the heart, stitch beyond the V, leave the needle on the inside edge, lift the presser foot, and turn. This makes a clean V.

As you approach the bottom, stitch to the very edge, leave the needle in the fabric on the outside, and turn.

The more you practice machine appliqué, the more improved your technique will become. Learning to feed the fabric flowing with the curves is a real art.

One last trick: Whenever I can, I put thin needlepunch behind the project. Then as I stitch through, the shape has more dimension.

Hand Appliqué

Hand appliqué is a technique used to apply a fabric shape to a background. A seam allowance of ⅛″ to ¼″ must be left on the outside edge of the design to turn under.

The shape can be traced with a sharp pencil on the right side of the fabric. This serves as a guide

in turning under the edges. I also like to machine stitch the sewing line in a short basting stitch. This acts as a guide in turning the edges under. A scant ¼″ is all that's needed for a seam allowance. The seam lines are essential to accurate hand appliqué. Be sure to choose thread that matches the appliqué.

For ease in shaping pieces, clip the inside curves to almost the seam line. You will find it easier to turn under about one inch of the edge at a time with your fingers holding it with your thumb and forefinger and stitch to that point. Let your needle work the seam allowance under smoothly as you stitch.

Appliqué stitches should be close together and pulled snugly to achieve a smooth line. Trim away excess background fabric from behind the appliqué. This eliminates the problem of layers showing through and the problems of quilting through extra layers of fabric. The blindstitch and whipstitch, two popular appliqué stitches, are shown. *Blindstitch* thread travels behind the base fabric (needle comes from outside in).

Whipstitch thread remains next to the edge of the appliqué.

Freezer Paper Method

Freezer paper appliqué is a very accurate method for turning the raw edges under in hand appliqué. Because of the rounded shape of the heart top and the center V shape, raw edges can be difficult to turn under evenly.

1. Using freezer paper (from the grocery store), cut out the finished shape you desire.

2. Press the paper shape with the waxy side of the paper to the *wrong* side of the fabric using a hot iron. This will bond the paper to the fabric.

3. Trim away excess fabric, leaving a seam allowance of a scant ¼" around the paper shape. Clip to the center, within three or four threads.

CLIP

4. Pin the heart shape to the background fabric or use a glue stick to hold it in place.

5. Using thread that matches the appliqué, begin stitching on a side. The needle should come up and catch the appliqué shape, then travel directly to the wrong side of the backing fabric.

6. Let the needle work the raw edges under the paper as you travel. The firmness of the paper creates a clean edge.

7. As you approach the V at the top of the heart, run the needle from left to right along the V.

Then take tiny stitches close together.

8. For a defined point at the bottom of the heart, turn up the point of the fabric, then turn in each side and stitch it in place.

9. Once the heart is stitched in place, turn over the background fabric. You will see the heart stitching line. Using sharp, pointed-tip scissors, cut away the fabric inside the heart shape about ¼" from the stitching line. Gently, pull out the freezer paper. It can be reused.

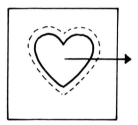

Dimensional Hearts
Batting Method

This method gives the appliqué shape a flat padded look. I use it for 1" hearts as well as larger ones. The technique is the same no matter what the size.

Trace the heart shape on the back side of the fabric. Put two layers of fabric right sides together on top of a piece of 3 oz. bonded quilt batting. Pin the layers together. Machine stitch on the pencil line through all three layers. Trim excess fabric and batting to a scant ¼" from the stitching line. Clip the V and point.

Look at the diagram; you'll see that one layer of the heart is slit, just enough to turn it to the right

side. An unsharpened pencil or chopstick will help you push out the stubborn sides. (The slit should be cut before you stitch the hearts together.)

SLIT

Very lightly, press the heart shape. Too much heat from the iron will melt the batting and make it stiff. Hand tack the slit shut.

Stuffing Method

Stuffing hearts is a little like making tiny heart-shaped pillows. Stitch the two fabrics together, clip, turn, and press. Usually a small section on the side is left open for stuffing. A good quality stuffing will be more resilient through use and will lump up less.

Use an unsharpened pencil or chopstick to poke little pieces of stuffing into the heart. Pull apart small pieces of stuffing, then put a small amount in at a time, pushing it to the far side. By using small amounts of stuffing, you can adequately stuff the tiny places. This takes patience, but you will be happy you took the time.

Pieced Hearts
Curved

Curves in patchwork add a softened dimension to all the angles. Maybe that's why I'm so fond of hearts and fans. Curves within the heart shape fascinate me, though they must be simple if you wish to machine piece.

Draw the curves on the desired heart shape. Make a smaller drawing of the shape for future reference.

1. Mark each section with a number or letter, then add notches at the interior seams.

2. Cut the pattern apart and place pieces on the right side of your fabric choices.

3. Mark with a pencil where the notches are.

4. Cut around each, leaving a ¼" seam allowance.

5. Stitch A to B, B to C, and so on. On the inside curves, snip slightly.

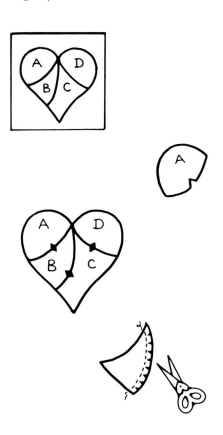

For good results, match the notches and pin in place. Sew slowly, easing as you go. Press the seam the way it wants to go.

In the "Curved Heart" quilt block in the sampler, the curves were designed so the block would fit together when one heart is right side up and one is upside down. The center section moves like a ribbon. The three blocks chained together in "Victorian Hearts" also illustrate this.

Heart Grids
"Checkerboard Heart" is an example of a grided heart shape, as is the heart on the border of the sampler quilt on the cover. Both were developed from a square grid. By enlarging or reducing the squares, the design can change.

In the *Checkerboard Hearts* wall quilt, the square grid was treated like a nine-patch, giving an entirely different look from the block in the sampler quilt. Whenever possible, sew several strips together and cut across them to form your square.

Crazy Patch
This is my very favorite way of doing patchwork. I like the look of the angles and scraps of fabric tied together with ribbons and embroidery. Crazy patch can be planned two different ways. One is to draw the design first on paper, then make templates. This method is detailed in Part Four, "Crazy at Heart." The second method is more spontaneous. Gather up a palette of scraps that work together colorwise. You could choose several shades of one color, a smaller amount of a second color, and a sparkle. The sparkle can be a contrasting color such as a brighter or darker tone, or it can be a change in texture like velveteen, lace, ribbon, brocade, etc. The fabrics don't all have to be cotton.

Once your palette is selected, place it on a table, walk out of the room, return, and quickly glance at the scraps. Your mind will tell you if the combination works or not. You may have to revise.

Trace on muslin the heart shape you want to crazy patch. Cut it out, adding ¼" seam allowance.

Look at the diagram, then proceed step by step. Remember, no two crazy patches will be exactly alike unless you use the template

method. Be brave and just let yourself go.

1. Place an odd-shaped piece on the heart. Pin in place. (Maybe it's a special flower or piece of lace.)

2. Pull a second fabric. I make sure Piece 2 has something in common with Piece 1. They need to be color friends. Place the raw edges together. Machine stitch through all three layers. Flip the fabric over.

3. Trim off the excess of the second strip so it follows the first strip. See dotted lines in diagram.

4. Add the third piece on any side. It doesn't matter. Eventually you work yourself to the outer edges.

5. If ribbon or lace is to be added, pin it on a strip before you add another. Then the raw edges are tucked under.

6. Trim off the excess fabric back to the muslin when you're finished.

I use this method to experiment with fabric combinations, then make them into heart pincushions for friends. As you practice this technique, you'll get more and more innovative. The crazy patch quilt in Photo 2 was done this way. It began when I was demonstrating crazy patch in class. One thing lead to another, and it ended up being a wall quilt with crazy patch border.

Piecing

Strips to Squares

This fast and accurate method of making squares is my very favorite. It was used to make the tiny blue-and-white checks in the strip-pieced heart in the sampler. Because you are working with strips, small squares are easy to come by.

1. To determine the width of the strips, take the finished width desired and add ½″ seam allowance. (Example: 1″ finished and ½″ seam allowance equals a 1½″ cut strip.) The length of the strip is determined by the number of squares you need. To determine length, take the cut size times the number needed.

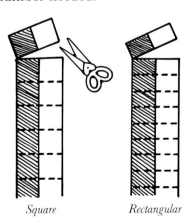

Square   *Rectangular*

2. Stitch the two strips together. Press the seam toward the darker fabric.

3. Cut across the strips (as the dotted lines show) with a rotary cutter or scissors. The width of the cut is determined in Step 1.

4. If you want rectangular pieces, make narrower cuts.

5. Chain these together to form one long strip.

6. Or, if you want a four-patch block, stitch together as shown.

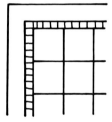

This method is great for making borders on quilts where you want to incorporate lots of fabrics.

Triangles

I use a template if I don't have very many pieces to cut, but I'd rather use the bias strip method; it's so fast and accurate. If you need tiny triangles such as those on a feathered star quilt, it works great.

1. To determine the width of the bias strip, measure the square template from corner to corner and include seam allowances. Divide this measurement by 2, and then add ½″.

Example:
$$4'' \div 2 = 2'' + \tfrac{1}{2}'' = 2\tfrac{1}{2}''$$

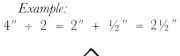

2. Cut two strips on the bias the width determined above.

3. Sew the strips together, with ¼″ seam allowance.

4. Press the seams open or toward the darker fabric.

5. Place the square template on the strip, making sure the template line from corner to corner matches the seam line.

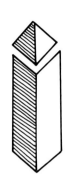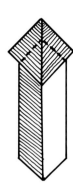

6. Make a cut on each side of the template as shown.

7. Turn the template around and position to cut the other two sides. To determine the length, go back to Step 1 and look at your measurement from corner to corner.

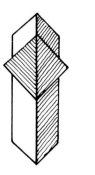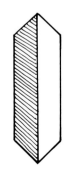

8. Continue this process until the blocks are all cut. The leftover side pieces can be used for borders or other projects.

Embellishments

Added touches such as embroidered French knots, bows, buttons, cording, and prairie points all help to create a finished look to your project.

Embroidery

Embroidery can be an outline to define an area or an added texture to embellish a motif. We have used embroidery in a gentle way to further emphasize a design concept. Here are some basic—though important—embroidery stitches.

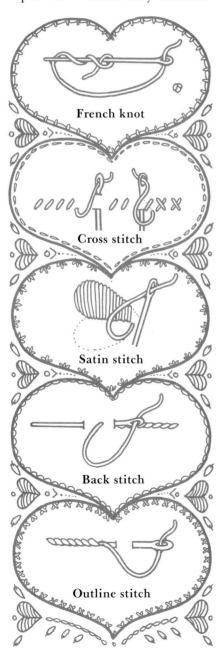

French knot

Cross stitch

Satin stitch

Back stitch

Outline stitch

Ribbons and Buttons

Ribbons tied in bows are most often used in our projects. Today's ribbons are washable and hold up well with use. Our bows were attached with French knots, which can be made of either embroidery floss or regular sewing thread.

To make a dramatic bow shape, allow a little extra fullness when shaping the bow. A knot can be tied to the center or it can be shaped without a knot. Place pins in the bow where the knots will hold it to the fabric, leaving loops or fullness. The ribbon can be turned and twisted.

The *Victorian Hearts* quilt and box use ribbons in a subtle way, creating a textural mood. Choose a variety of colors and ribbon widths. Place the ribbons first, before buttons are stitched on. In the diagram, a ribbon loop is made, trimmed off, then stitched directly to the fabric.

Two or three loops can be formed with smaller ribbons. They almost look like leaves.

Bows can be formed and stitched in the middle, leaving long streamers.

Or, loop several colors or ribbons leaving long streamers.

Buttons are stitched in place with double thread. Knot the thread after each button. As I add buttons, I let them overlap and cluster together almost like a bouquet. In the projects here, old pearl buttons were used. The back of the button is the imperfect side; it usually has more texture and color. A garden effect is created with the loops of ribbon and clustered buttons along with the patchwork.

Cording

In this technique, cording is encased in fabric and used around the edge of designs. Most of the appliqué heart pieces and pillows have cording of some kind. Like a mat on a painting, cording helps to define the shape. Store-bought bias tape can be used to make cording, but often it's difficult to find the correct color. Handmade bias tape is the answer; here are instructions.

1. Begin with two squares of fabric. Cut them diagonally.

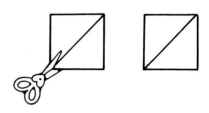

2. Stitch these four triangles together.

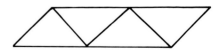

3. With a ruler, mark cutting lines. They need to be wide enough to fit over the cording, plus ½".

4. Connect the two ends of the bias strip as shown. Note Line A meets Line B, Line B meets C, and so on.

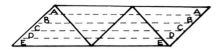

5. Starting at the top, cut the tape apart along the lines.

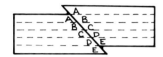

To make cording fit your machine with a zipper foot: Place the cording inside the bias strip, making sure seam allowances are inside. Stitch through the layers of fabric with the zipper foot fitting snugly next to the cording.

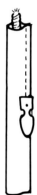
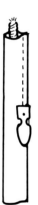

Prairie Points
Prairie points are folded squares of fabric that project out as a triangle shape from the edge of a design. They were used in ''Desert Bloom'' to create the top edge of the heart shape.
1. Fold a small square of fabric diagonally.
2. Then bring each corner to the center.
3. Place in an open seam; sew. The bottom will be trimmed off.

The Finishing Touch
Borders
Borders on a quilt or pillow act like a frame in a painting; they're a necessary finishing touch. They can be a single fabric or a combination of fabrics. Individual instructions are given in each project for border design and construction.

Mitering Corners
Mitered corners have a diagonal seam running from the inside seam to the outside edge. When using stripes, mitered corners are especially effective.
1. Stitch strip to within ¼″ from the raw edge of the quilt. Whatever the width of the strip, leave that amount of fabric at the end of the strip (for a 2″ wide strip, leave 2″ excess at the end of the strip).

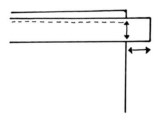

2. Leave the same amount of fabric at the end of the next strip. Pin to quilt. Start stitching (at the same spot you left off) through quilt and binding only. Push seam allowances aside.

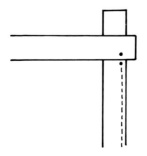

3. Press seams toward binding, letting strips overlap each other. Draw a line with a ruler from the stitching corner to where strips overlap.

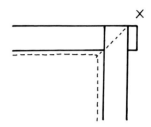

4. Pull both pieces of binding to the back of the quilt and stitch together on the pencil line on the binding only.

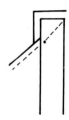

Marking the Quilt Top
Everyone has their favorite marking method for quilting. My method varies, depending on the project. Whatever method you choose, TEST IT FIRST. There's nothing worse than having the markings become permanent when that was not your intention. Here are some different marking methods:
• Lead pencil—an art gum eraser can remove stubborn pencil lines.
• Blue pens—can be difficult to remove if there is a finish on the fabric.
• Dressmaker's carbon—most brands are washable so be sure your fabric is too.

• Chalk—some will rub off before you are finished quilting.

• ¼"-wide masking tape—don't leave it on the quilt too long. It deteriorates and leaves a gummy residue.

• Silver pencil (my favorite)—marks lightly and rubs off as you quilt.

For templates, I use my ruler for straight lines. If the fabric is light enough, I tape it to a window, placing the quilting design behind it. You can see through the fabric to trace the lines. Or cut the shapes and trace around them.

Quilting

Quilting is the process in which the batting is sandwiched between the quilt top and backing and stitches are taken through the three layers to secure them. These can be hand or machine stitches. Sometimes I machine quilt in the seams, then hand quilt the open space.

Machine quilting has become more and more acceptable with quilters having less and less time to quilt. For details on the process, see Barbara Johannah's excellent book on machine quilting; it's listed in the Bibliography.

Use monofilament thread in the top and thread matching the quilt back in the bobbin. Pin or baste the quilt layers together securely. Roll up the area of the quilt you are not quilting so it can fit in the arm of the machine. Set the stitch length to ten stitches per inch. Feed the quilt through evenly; take your time. Working on a large table helps. Your quilt won't pull as it goes through the machine. Pull thread ends to the quilt back and tie.

Hand quilting is the use of small hand stitches to hold the three layers together. There's something so arresting about beautifully done hand quilting. Doing hand quilt-

ing is a little like therapy to me. I like to use a frame or hoop. Knot a single thread and pull it through the top layer of fabric so it disappears. Sometimes you need to scratch the knot to get it through the fabric. Scratch and pull the thread at the same time. The needle should travel as straight as it can through the fabric and come up straight. The first few stitches will be awkward. It usually takes me about 15 minutes to really get into the rhythm of quilting.

Smaller, more compact stitches are possible with thinner batting. My preference is 3 oz. bonded batting or Cotton Classic™. If I'm going to hand quilt, I like nice, even small stitches.

Binding

Binding needs to be at least 1½" wide. It can be on the straight of grain or on the bias. It is attached like the borders by machine, turned under ¼", pulled to the wrong side of the quilt, and stitched in place by hand or machine.

To turn the corners, a mitered fold creates a clean edge. Before turning under the ¼" seam allowance, turn under the corner as shown. Press. Then turn under the edges ¼", and stitch.

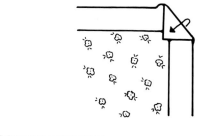
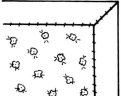

Some of the quilts such as *Hearts and Vines* don't use binding. The

batting and backing are trimmed to ½" from the front of the quilt. Then the front fabric is turned and stitched to the back by hand as described above.

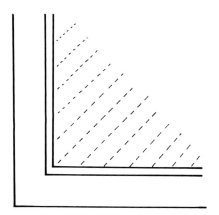

Ruffles

Ruffles can be single thickness of fabric or double. To make a single thickness ruffle, determine the width of the finished ruffle and add 1". This is the total width needed. The length is determined by measuring around the project, then doubling that measurement. Hem the top edge by turning under ¼" twice so no raw edges show, then machine topstitch. Gather the lower edge ½" from the raw edge using a basting stitch. Pull bobbin thread and space gathers evenly around the edge. Enclose in a seam.

To determine the width of a double ruffle, take the finished width, double it, and add 1". Fold the ruffle in half lengthwise and press. Then gather.

If you have a long ruffle and are concerned about the gathering threads breaking, zigzag over fishing leader or monofilament thread. Then just pull up the monofilament thread.

Backing Hearts

Sometimes you may find yourself making a tiny heart, and you don't want to leave the side open for turning and stuffing. Sharon Hultgren, a student, reminded me of a clever technique.

1. Cut out two backs for the heart shape. Fold each in half lengthwise.

2. Place the two backs on the right side of the heart shape. Stitch around the entire edge. Clip. Turn to the right side through the center back.

3. Hand stitch the folds together after stitching.

Turn to right side

Seeds of heart
Stitched with care
Bloom year upon year---
A perennial garden
in which to share---

Marina

Bibliography

Anderson, Marina. *Crayon Creations.* Yours Truly, Inc., Atlanta, GA, 1984.

Anderson, Marina. *Crayon Design Workbook.* Yours Truly, Inc., Atlanta, GA, 1985.

Dietrich, Mimi. *Happy Endings.* That Patchwork Place, Bothell, WA, 1988.

Fons, Marianne. *Fine Feathers.* C & T Publishing, Lafayette, CA, 1987.

Johannah, Barbara. *Continuous Curve Quilting.* C & T Publishing, Lafayette, CA, 1982.

Lawson, Suzy. *Band Boxes Patterns and Kits.* Amity Publications, Cottage Grove, OR, 1987.

McCloskey, Marsha and Martin, Nancy. *A Dozen Variables.* That Patchwork Place, Bothell, WA, 1987.

Montano, Judith. *The Crazy Quilt Handbook.* C & T Publishing, Lafayette, CA, 1986.

Schaffner, Cynthia and Klein, Susan. *Folk Hearts.* Alfred A. Knopf, New York, 1984.

Thompson, Terry and Brannock, Linda. *Hearts for American Country Homes.* Quilt Country, Kansas City, MO, 1984.

Wells, Jean. *Fans.* C & T Publishing, Lafayette, CA, 1987.

Wells, Jean. *Patchworthy Apparel.* Burdett Publications, Atlanta, GA, 1978.